FOR ORGANS, PIANOS & ELECTRONIC KEYBOARDS

E-Z PLAY TODAY
177

I'll Be Seeing You
50 SONGS OF WORLD WAR II

D1451147

Many of the photographs in this publication are
War Information Office photographs from the
Historical Photo Collection of the
Milwaukee Public Library.

This publication is not for sale in
the E.C. and/or Australia
or New Zealand.

ISBN 0-7935-5075-0

7777 W. BLUEMOUND RD. P.O. BOX 13819 MILWAUKEE, WI 53213

Hasten the Homecoming

FROM THE SATURDAY EVENING POST COVER PAINTING
BY NORMAN ROCKWELL

BUY VICTORY BONDS

FOR ORGANS, PIANOS & ELECTRONIC KEYBOARDS

E-Z PLAY TODAY 177

I'll Be Seeing You
50 SONGS OF WORLD WAR II

AMERICA AT WAR:
The Home Front

by Elaine Schmidt

★ ★ ★ **1941** ★ ★ ★

As the forties began, the depression was over, but much of the country had not recovered from the economic devastation of the previous decade. Many Americans were still unemployed, underfed, and poorly housed. As the nation struggled back toward economic health, news of the wars in Europe and Asia caused grim speculation about what was to come. When Congress passed the Selective Service Act, establishing the nation's first peacetime draft, many saw it as the first step toward war. Men between 20 and 36 were required to register. Marriage license bureaus throughout the country were flooded with business as men sought

The USS Shaw burns after being bombed in the attack on Pearl Harbor.

deferments through marriage. A sudden increase in the national birthrate 9-10 months after the Selective Service Act was passed indicated that many saw family as a sure deferment. Ill-prepared for the sudden surge of conscriptees,

the Army struggled with housing, uniform and weapons shortages. Draftees often fought war games in civilian clothes, using mop handles as rifles while sacks of flour flew through the air as mock artillery fire. At the same time,

many in the country felt that the wars in Europe and Asia were not America's business. Isolation, they felt, was the answer.

Left: *A fire watcher during black-out in New York City.*

Center: *A demonstration of how to put up black-out curtains.*

Right: *Rubber salvage drive, led by the Boy Scouts and Boys Clubs.*

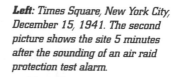

𝒜ttitudes changed instantly when, on December 7, 1941, the Japanese launched a devastating surprise attack on the U.S. Naval base at Pearl Harbor, Hawaii, killing some 3,000 Americans. Within days, young American men were flocking to enlist in all branches of service, with all thoughts of deferments forgotten. The once vocal isolationists were silenced by the cry, "Remember Pearl Harbor." Four days after the Pearl Harbor attack, Hitler's Germany and Mussolini's Italy declared war on the United States. National outrage over Pearl Harbor galvanized the country. Patriotism and the desire to help the war effort were felt from coast to coast. The nation prepared for attack. As the war effort got underway, in New York City tall buildings dimmed their lights to avoid silhouetting U.S. ships for enemy submarines. Armed soldiers patrolled both coasts and Washington, D.C. Black-outs and brown-outs were in effect throughout the country, particularly on the coasts. Rubber rationing, the first of many wartime rationing regulations, was announced by year's end. When President Roosevelt asked the country for its scrap rubber, the Boy Scouts answered by collecting some 54,000 tons in the next year.

The popular culture of 1941 quickly shifted to war-themed entertainment, including song hits like the Andrews Sisters' "Boogie Woogie Bugle Boy," "I Don't Want to Set the World on Fire," recorded by Tommy Tucker (and later by the Ink Spots), and "Kiss the Boys Goodbye," recorded by Tommy Dorsey, with a vocal by Connie Haines. Movies released that year included the Frank Capra classic *Meet John Doe* (starring Gary Cooper and Barbara Stanwyck), *Suspicion* (starring Cary Grant and Joan Fontaine), and *How Green Was My Valley* (starring Walter Pidgeon, Maureen O'Hara, and Roddy McDowall). *The Lady Eve* (starring Henry Fonda and Barbara Stanwyck) was one of the last of the sophisticated romantic comedies, a style of movie that flourished in the late 30s. Wartime brought new emotions in audiences, and the days of madcap, urbane, wisecracking sophisticates in smart clothes (all hallmarks of 30s movies) were quickly giving way to a new aesthetic.

★★★ 1942 ★★★

The opening of 1942 was heralded with prayers for a swift end to the war. There was an immediate ban on the sale of new cars and trucks. Factories hastily re-tooled for production of military materials. Families moved to cities that offered defense-related jobs, ending lingering unemployment woes. Victory gardens were planted in front and back yards of homes. Lowered "victory speeds" were enacted, and ride-sharing encouraged drivers to conserve gasoline. Scrap and recycling drives collected metal, tin, paper, and even cooking grease for use in defense production. Plastics began to replace metal in every possible area of civilian life. Clocks were turned ahead one hour in February as "war time" (later known as Daylight Savings Time) went into effect. Gasoline rationing began in May, soon followed by coffee and sugar rationing. As silk stockings became a casualty of the war, many women simply drew "seams" on bare legs with eyebrow pencils. Wartime regulations dictated women's hem lengths (shorter) and number of pockets. Hoods, coat cuffs, zippers, and metal fastenings were banned. Sales of women's trousers increased by five to ten times over the previous year. Men were restricted in coat lengths and pant leg widths. Cuffs, pleats, tucks, and overlapping waistbands were no longer allowed.

A female work force was stepping forward to fill positions vacated as men left for the war. Asheville, N.C. was served by an all-female fire department. Minority women entered the factories and shops in significant numbers for the first time. When the Armed Services opened their recruiting station doors to women in May, more than 13,000 appeared to register. Eventually more than 143,000 women would serve in the WAC (Women's Army Corps). In addition, the Navy, Marines and Coast Guard would add women's units. Women filled Stateside military positions as mechanics, drivers, cooks, and pilots. The 93rd infantry, an all black combat division, was organized.

Hollywood produced some 80 war movies in 1942, while sending its stars off to the real war. Among those in the military were Gene Autry, Douglas Fairbanks, James Stewart, Spencer Tracy, Darryl Zanuck, Frank Capra, and Clark Gable. Hollywood's women joined the effort as well, entertaining troops, endorsing at-home war efforts and selling war bonds. Glamorous Carole Lombard and 20 others died in a TWA transport crash, while on a bond-selling tour. The inspirational hit film *Mrs. Miniver* (starring Greer Garson) told the story of a British family coping with the German bombing and its devastating results. The enduring film most associated with the era, *Casablanca*, was released in 1942. Cheerful films (sometimes a little self-consciously so) flourished as an antidote to the war.

Above: *A Japanese-American family in an internment camp in Manzanar, California.*

Below: *The Sullivan brothers of Fredericksburg, Iowa, insisted on serving together in the Navy. All five were lost as the USS Juneau was sunk in the Pacific on November 14, 1942. It was the most severe patriotic sacrifice by any American family since the Civil War, and inspired a movie about the brothers. As a response to the tragedy, the armed forces created the policy that brothers could not serve together in the same divisions.*

the five Sullivan brothers "missing in action" off the Solomons

THEY DID THEIR PART

*F*ilms like *Holiday Inn* (where Bing Crosby introduced "White Christmas," a powerfully sentimental wartime song), *Yankee Doodle Dandy* (a patriotic biography of George M. Cohan starring James Cagney), *Woman of the Year* (the first teaming of Katharine Hepburn and Spencer Tracy), *Road to Morocco* (Bob Hope, Bing Crosby and Dorothy Lamour), and *The Palm Beach Story* (Joel McCrea and Claudette Colbert) were popular. Typical of musicals of the time, *A Star Spangled Rhythm* packed stars, songs and comic sketches into a thin plot. Movie houses were still the center of most communities, not only for the double feature entertainment and cartoons, but also for the newsreels of the war.

Wartime had thoroughly changed the hit parade, and 1942's hit songs included "The White Cliffs of Dover," "Praise the Lord and Pass the Ammunition," "I Left My Heart at the Stage Door Canteen" and the biggest hit of all, "White Christmas." War books included, *Train from Berlin* and *Victory Through Air Power*. The year's best-sellers included Pearl S. Buck's *Dragon Steel,* and Lloyd C. Douglas' *The Robe*. Irving Berlin's revue *This Is the Army,* with all-soldier cast, opened on Broadway on July 4 as a benefit for the Army Emergency Relief Fund (the show later toured the country). Berlin himself stopped the show each evening with his rendition of "Oh How I Hate to Get Up in the Morning."

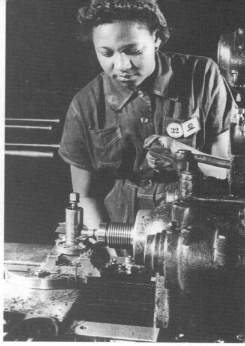

*Left: All modes of transportation were overcrowded during the war. Here's an experiment with the "stand-sit" seat in an effort to conserve passenger space. It didn't catch on. **Right:** African-American women entered the factory workplace in significant numbers for the first time during the war. This woman is working in an airplane factory.*

★ ★ ★ ★ ★ ★ ★ ★ ★ ★ ★ ★ **1943** ★ ★ ★ ★ ★ ★ ★ ★ ★ ★ ★ ★

*O*n the home front, 1943 brought more shortages and ration restrictions. Butter, cheese, flour, fish, and canned goods joined the list of rationed items. Shoes were rationed at three pairs a year, and the rubber shortage curtailed the manufacture of new sneakers. The shortage of paper for Christmas cards led families to fashion their own cards from brown grocery bags. Long store lines became a fact of life. Long distance calls were limited to five minutes in duration, and the gasoline shortage forced cabbies to carry as many fares at one time as their cabs would hold. In efforts to forget their worries, if only for an evening, Americans were dancing everything from the fox trot, polka, rhumba, samba, and waltz, to the wildly popular jitterbug and Lindy hop. Local variations on the Lindy hop took on such names as the Jersey hop, flea hop, job walk, victory hop and "Praise the Lord and Pass the Ammunition" dance. Jive, a "danceable jazz," became popular.

Store owners kept two containers for ration stamps, one for red and one for blue.

*C*ivilian women wore tailored suits nearly everywhere, and overcoats took on military names like the "Officer's Style" (long coat), and the "Seaman's" (short coat). Teenage girls sported rolled-up jeans, shirt-tails, mixed shoes and rag curlers. Teenage "hep cats" wore the Zoot Suit, which featured a long single button jacket with broad, padded shoulders and peaked lapels. Trousers were high-waisted, baggy at the knees, and narrow at the ankles. A wide silk tie, colored or striped shirt, a knee-length key chain and broad-brimmed hat were Zoot essentials. Throughout the country, men shaved off moustaches because of their fascist associations.

The nation was reading *A Tree Grows in Brooklyn* by Betty Smith, and William Saroyan's *The Human Comedy*. The war prompted such book titles as *God Is My Co-Pilot*, *Seven Came Through*, and *Here Is Your War*. Irving Berlin could be seen in the film version of his musical *This Is the Army*. Other movies to hit the screen were *Shadow of a Doubt* (a Hitchcock yarn starring Teresa Wright and Joseph Cotten), *Heaven Can Wait* (with Gene Tierney and Don Ameche), and *Lassie Come Home* (starring Roddy McDowall). Musicals on the country's screens included the Alice Faye picture *The Gang's All Here*, *Stormy Weather* (with Lena Horne) and *Girl Crazy* (Mickey Rooney and Judy Garland).

Right: Understanding rationing regulations kept customers and store owners busy. [photo: Office of Price Administration, National Archives]

On Broadway, the opening of *Oklahoma!* began a new era in American musical theater, the era of the often sentimental book-musical, as opposed to the more casually conceived entertainments often found on Broadway previously.

Songwriters were becoming more creative in their attempts to fit wartime sentiments into a 32 bar popular song. Some of the top song hits of 1943 were "Do Nothin' Till You Hear from Me" (recorded by Duke Ellington, Stan Kenton, and Woody Herman), "Have I Stayed Away Too Long" (Perry Como), and "You'd Be So Nice to Come Home To" (recorded by Dinah Shore).

The year saw one interesting musical development on radio. Because of a musicians' strike over revenues, for a time all instrumental music was banned from broadcast, leaving the airwaves to the sound of a cappella voices. Typical of this time, famous singers recorded new arrangements of standards backed up by a small choral group.

Above Right: Actress Joan Blondell at a North Atlantic base while on tour with a USO show.

Right: The Aircraft Warning Service.

Far Right: The speed limit was lowered to conserve gas and rubber. [Library of Congress]

VICTORY SPEED 35 MILES

*I*n 1944 the nation was shocked by details of the mass-murders of citizens by the German military at Birkenau and Auschwitz. Germany introduced the pilotless, "robot" bomb, and the highly destructive V-2, a supersonic rocket, doing terrible damage to British cities. For Americans, the new weapons meant stricter black-out restrictions, and a heightened fear of attack. 3.5 million American women were at work beside some 6 million men on defense industry assembly lines. The composite character of the typical working woman was nicknamed "Rosie the Riveter," and these working women enjoyed a new personal and financial independence, spurred on by the example of activist-first lady Eleanor Roosevelt. Salvage drives were still in full swing. Nearly half the country's war needs in steel, tin, and paper were provided by civilian salvage efforts.

It was a boom year for the arts. American artists found a new demand for their paintings in the absence of European works. Hollywood experienced the best year to

Above: Army nurses somewhere in the South Pacific.

date in box office receipts, grossing nearly $2,000,000,000. Movie offerings ranged from the requisite war films, to nostalgia and thrillers. *Follow the Boys*, a film intended as entertainment for American troops abroad, featured a virtual parade of stars. The film was a tribute to the Hollywood Victory Committee and contained actual footage of stars entertaining the troops. American films were in demand again in the recently liberated areas of Europe. Among the new movie hits of 1944 were *The Lodger* (starring Merle Oberon and George Sanders), *Going My Way* (Bing Crosby), the film noir classic *Double Indemnity* (Fred MacMurray and Barbara Stanwyck), *Gaslight* (Ingrid Bergman), *Meet Me in St. Louis* (Judy Garland), and *Cover Girl* (Gene Kelly and Rita Hayworth). Broadway had a box office boom as well, with plays like *Harvey*, *I Remember Mama*, and *Ten Little Indians*. The year's

Below: Contralto Marian Anderson at the Department of the Interior Auditorium for the dedication of a mural commemorating her free public concert at the Lincoln Memorial, Easter Sunday, 1939. The concert was a powerful rallying statement, attended by tens of thousands, against discrimination, of which she herself was a victim. The DAR had denied her the right to sing at their meeting.

stage musicals included *Carmen Jones*, *Song of Norway*, *On the Town*, *Bloomer Girl*, and the still-running *Oklahoma!*

Paper shortages prompted publishers to experiment with "soft-cover" books. The nation was reading W. Somerset Maugham's *The Razor's Edge*, Bob Hope's *I Never Left Home*, and

"THE GIRL HE LEFT BEHIND" IS STILL BEHIND HIM
She's a WOW

A Woman Ordnance Worker recruiting poster. [Franklin D. Roosevelt Library]

To Have and to Hold!

WAR BONDS

OFFICIAL U. S. TREASURY POSTER

WFD 891

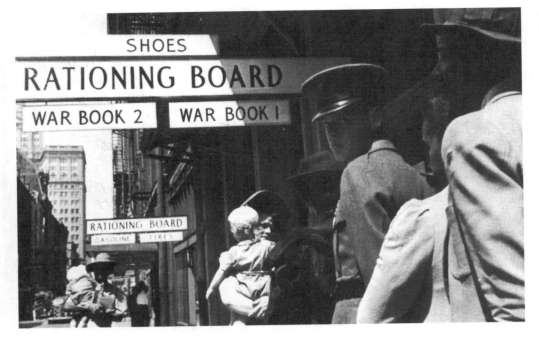

SHOES
RATIONING BOARD
WAR BOOK 2   WAR BOOK 1

RATIONING BOARD
GASOLINE   TIRES

Margaret Landon's *Anna and the King of Siam*. With many professional baseball players still in the service and the quality of the nation's pastime greatly diminished, college football became the nation's sport of choice. The silly cartoon and slogan "Kilroy was here" began appearing in graffiti both at home and abroad. Among the top radio shows of the year were: "Fibber McGee and Molly," "Abbott and Costello," and "Jack Benny." As fashion designers continued fleeing Europe, New York had become the world's fashion capitol. Still working under war restrictions, designers introduced the three-quarter-length box coat, suits with false fronts, chignons, pillbox hats, and berets. The revolutionary idea of "separates," or interchangeable clothes, was introduced.

The year began with an unusual music story. ASCAP, the organization for collecting royalties for composers, lyricists, and publishers, had a rift with the radio industry over royalties. On January 1 the radio stations of the country declared a self-imposed ban on all ASCAP titles, which included the

material of all the mainstream, established songwriters of the day, including every single hit song of time! Determined to go their way without ASCAP, the broadcasters organized their own administrative organization, Broadcast Music Inc., and sought out unsigned writers. This was a great boost to music previously ignored by the respectable ranks of Broadway-oriented ASCAP, music by minorities, bluegrass and country music, and regional musicians who had not yet made it big. The dispute was resolved within several weeks, but the effects of this period were lasting. (BMI continued to grow and was the major player in the development of rock and rhythm and blues in coming years.)

Hit songs included "Spring Will Be a Little Late This Year," and the quintessential song of the era "I'll Be Seeing You." The song had actually been around since 1939, having been introduced in an unsuccesful Broadway show entitled *Right This Way*. Though not actually written during wartime, the lyrics and mood of the song seem to perfectly capture the emotions of millions of American couples separated by the war. The song hit number 1 ten different times, the most successful recording was by Frank Sinatra with Tommy Dorsey. Also during this year, Americans mourned the death of Major Glenn Miller, the famous big band leader and director of the U.S. Air Force Band, who was lost on a flight from London to Paris.

Many Hollywood celebrities served in the military, including Major James Stewart, here receiving the Air Medal after completing 10 missions over Germany. He was later promoted to Colonel. [U.S. Air Force]

Right: *A Hospital Train with U.S. army nurses, pulling out of a station with wounded from the northern Italian front.*

Facing page: *Volunteer seamstresses work on large American flags for recruitment flag poles.*

★★★★ 1945 ★★★★

The America that had been drawn into World War II in 1941 no longer existed by the war's end in 1945. The world itself was a vastly different place. In unleashing atomic weapons on Japan, still the only military use of such weapons on the planet, the U.S. ushered in a new era of military might and danger. By August the war was over, with the Allied forces finally victorious. America's era of isolation was also over. The war's end marked the beginning of the U.S.'s reign as a major world power, and it began an on-going involvement in foreign affairs and aid to nations in need. The man most responsible for the victory, President Franklin Roosevelt, did not see the war's end. He died in Warm Springs, GA, on the 83rd day of his fourth term as President.

Home-life was also radically changed from the pre-war years. Returning service men intensified the already acute housing shortage. A lack of materials and construction workers had held the country's home-building at a virtual standstill. Men returning from the war married in large numbers, and millions of couples were looking for houses that simply didn't exist. Many women who had taken on "men's" work during the war,

resented their post-war job losses, fighting "job discrimination on the basis of sex." During the war, many Americans had been making money for the first time since the depression. With few goods available for purchase, large nest eggs had accumulated. The war's end brought the desire to spend money, causing countless shortages. Stores were full of new wonders including frozen orange juice, ball point pens, aerosol spray insecticides, butane cigarette lighters, and Tupperware. Fashion designers developed the "rounded look" in women's fashion. Dresses and suits were fitted at the waist, neck, and wrist, with skirts belling over hips and thighs. Women's fashions emphasized prettiness and delicacy, in contrast to the padded shoulders and sharp lines of war-time fashions.

Above: *The Jitterbug. [Library of Congress]*

Left: *A small sized copy of the Statue of Liberty is erected in Times Square after the Japanese surrender is announced.*

News of the war's end was met with immediate, unbridled rejoicing. Americans on the home front vividly remember where they were and what they were doing at the moment they heard of Japan's surrender. Throughout the country people rushed into the streets, weeping, embracing, and shouting with joy and relief. Returning service men and women were greeted with parades, parties and celebrations. Even in celebration, there could be no denial of the nation's losses. Of the 16,200,000 Americans that had served in the armed forces, 292,000 had been

killed, and another 675,000 wounded. For those who returned uninjured, youth and innocence were casualties of the war. Despite devastating losses, Americans at home had responded whole-heartedly to the war effort and savored the heady feel of victory. Throughout the country a national sense of optimism reigned. No matter what hardships the coming years might hold, Americans were certain of their ability to overcome them. The nightmare was over. ■

Most families still relied on radio for in-home entertainment, and the average American still went to the movies on a weekly basis. The year's films began to be less occupied with war themes, and included *National Velvet* (with 12 year old Elizabeth Taylor), *State Fair* (the only Rodgers and Hammerstein musical written directly for film), *Mildred Pierce* (Joan Crawford), and *The Lost Weekend* (with Ray Milland as an alcoholic). Bing Crosby, Betty Grable, Spencer Tracy, Humphrey Bogart, Gary Cooper, Bob Hope, and Judy Garland were among the year's top box office draws. The up-beat, hopeful attitude of the country was captured in popular songs like: "Let It Snow!," "June Is Bustin' Out All Over," and "It's a Grand Night for Singing." Bepop, the complex style of Dizzy Gillespie, Miles Davis and Charlie ("Bird") Parker, was at its peak. The overall tone of the music on the Hit Parade had changed markedly since the

beginning of the decade. At the beginning of the war, the big bands and their leaders were the stars, and the solo singers were secondary in recordings and performances. This changed rather quickly, probably for many reasons, and by 1945 it was the singing stars who ruled the radio—Doris Day, Dinah Shore, Bing Crosby (who had always been popular), Perry Como, Jo Stafford, Kate Smith, and most important of all, Frank Sinatra. The style of the music had also changed, going

AMERICA AT WAR:
Major Events of World War II

★ ★ 1938 ★ ★

March 12. Germany invades Austria.

October 1. Germany occupies Czechoslovakia.

★ ★ 1939 ★ ★

March. Czechoslovakia ceases to exist as an independent nation. Bohemia and Moravia become German protectorates, and Slovakia comes under German control.

September 1. Germany invades Poland.

September 17. USSR invades Poland.

★ ★ 1940 ★ ★

April 9. Denmark is taken over by the Germans after virtually no resistance. Only 13 Danish lives were lost after the King declared that resistance was futile on the small, ill-equipped island. Nearly all Danish Jews were hidden and secretly sent to Sweden until the war's end.

April 9. Norway invaded by Germany. Heavy resistance allowed the royal family to escape, eventually settling in London.

May 10. Germany invades the Netherlands and Luxembourg. Many of the smaller countries were powerless to withstand German invasion. Germany saw them as posing little threat, and left occupying troops to maintain martial law.

May 12. Germans invade France.

May 28. Belgium surrenders to Germany.

June 11. Italy invades France.

June 14.. The Germans march into Paris; the government is moved to Tours.

Switzerland and the Vatican remained neutral throughout the war. The rest of Europe fell under Fascist rule, except Finland, which never fell to the Germans. It had lost territory to Russia in border battles of 1939 and 1940, and voluntarily allied itself with Germany in 1941 in order to fight Russia to regain the lost land.

July 25. U.S. ceases shipment of all strategic materials to Japan.

September 7. The London Blitz begins. Germans steadily bomb the British capital by night until May 10 of 1941.

September 16. Congress passes the Selective Service Act, creating America's first peace-time draft.

September 27. Japan officially joins the Axis alliance with Germany and Italy.

October 7. Germany invades Rumania.

October 28. Italy invades Greece.

November 5. Franklin Delano Roosevelt is elected President for a third term.

November 20. Hungary joins Hitler's Axis.

November 22. Rumania joins the Axis alliance.

★ ★ 1941 ★ ★

February 8. Bulgaria signs a military pact with Germany.

March 11. FDR signs the Lend-Lease Bill, allowing the U.S. "to send goods and munitions to democratic countries in return for services and goods."

March 16. The war in North Africa heats up, with British attacking Italian forces in Somaliland and Ethiopia.

April 11. The Office of Price Administration and Civilian Supply is established (known as OPA).

April 13. USSR and Japan sign a 5-year non-aggression pact.

April 17. Yugoslavia surrenders to Germany.

April 23. Greece surrenders to Germany.

May 1. U.S. Defense Savings Bonds and Stamps go on sale.

May 27. FDR declares an unlimited national emergency because of the momentum of events in Europe and Africa.

June 14. FDR orders all German and Italian assets in the U.S. frozen.

June 22. Germany, Italy and Rumania declare war on the USSR. Germany invades the USSR.

July 12. Britain and USSR sign military treaty assuring British aid to the Soviets.

July 26. U.S. officially stops all commercial trade with Japan.

August 9-12. British Prime Minister Winston Churchill and President Roosevelt meet secretly off Newfoundland to form the Atlantic Charter. The Charter's articles of agreement cover goals of the two countries before and after the war.

August 18. FDR signs the Selective Service Act Extension, expanding the military.

September 8. The German seige of Leningrad begins.

September 11. FDR issues an order to attack on sight all foreign vessels found operating in U.S. defensive waters.

October 17. U.S. destroyer Kearny is torpedoed and damaged by a German submarine off the coast of Iceland.

December 7. U.S. Naval base at Pearl Harbor, Hawaii, is hit by a surprise Japanese attack. Nineteen battleships are sunk or badly damaged; some 3000 Americans are killed. At the same time, Japanese forces attack Guam, Wake Island, the Philippines, and other strategic Pacific bases.

December 8. U.S. declares war on Japan. Japan declares war on U.S. and Britain. Japanese quickly bomb and invade Philippines, Wake Islands, Guam, Thailand, Malaya, Hong Kong.

December 11. Germany and Italy declare war against the U.S. Congress recognizes a state of war.

December 22. Wake Island falls to the Japanese.

December 27. Rubber rationing is announced by the OPA.

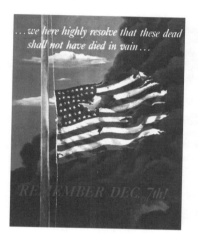

...we here highly resolve that these dead shall not have died in vain...

REMEMBER DEC. 7th!

★ ★ 1942 ★ ★

January 1. Declaration of the formation of the United Nations, signed by 26 countries, Washington, D.C.

January 2. Manila, Philippines, falls to the Japanese, forcing the retreat of U.S. and Philippine forces under General Douglas MacArthur.

Left: *The U.S. government financed production of war materials and its hugely enlarged military through the sale of war bonds to citizens.*

February. FDR signs the order for all Japanese-Americans to be gathered into "internment." The U.S. government would much later denounce the action . (On August 10, 1988, President Reagan signed a bill to publicly apologize and to compensate 120,000 survivors of the camps and their beneficiaries with $20,000 each, tax free.)

February 27-March 1. The U.S. suffers a major Naval defeat in the Battle of the Java Sea.

March 17. FDR orders MacArthur to concede Bataan (in the Philippines) in the face of an insurmountable Japanese offensive.

April 10. The "Bataan Death March" begins at dawn. American and Philippine prisoners are forced to march 85 miles in 6 days, with only 1 meal of rice for the entire week. Upwards of 5200 Americans and many more Filipinos die.

April 18. Major General James H. Doolittle commands the first air-raid on Tokyo.

Right: A Japanese-American grocer boldly proclaimed his nationality to all. The man was forced to close his business and enter a government run internment camp for the duration of the war. [War Relocation Authority, National Archives]

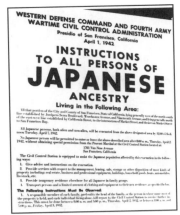

Above: Japanese-American relocation policy announcement, one of the darkest American memories of the war.

May 4-8. Battle of the Coral Sea. The Japanese sustain heavy losses from the U.S. Naval Air Force.

May 6. Corregidor falls to the Japanese.

May 14. Congress establishes the Women's Army Auxiliary Corps (WAAC).

May 24. Dwight D. Eisenhower is appointed commander of all U.S. troops in Europe.

June 4-8. Battle of Midway. Japan suffers heavy losses to relatively light U.S. losses.

July 30. Women Appointed for Voluntary Emergent Services (WAVES) is organized by the U.S. Naval Reserve.

August 7. U.S. Marines land on Guadalcanal, in the Solomon Islands. Fighting will continue here until February, 1943.

August 18. "Carlson's Raiders," a special guerilla warfare unit lead by Lt. Evans Carlson, defeat Japanese forces on Makin Island in 40 hours.

August 23. Battle of Stalingrad begins, continuing until January of 1944.

September 15. U.S. aircraft carrier Wasp is sunk off Guadalcanal.

November 7. U.S. forces begin landing in North Africa under the command of Lt. General Dwight D. Eisenhower. The first major Allied attack takes place the next day in Morocco and Algeria.

November 12-15. U.S. achieves major victory off Guadalcanal.

November 23. SPARS (Semper Paratus Always Ready Service), the women's branch of the Coast Guard, established.

★ ★ 1943 ★ ★

January 14. The Casablanca Conference. Allied officials, including Roosevelt and Churchill, meet in Morocco and agree to plan for a 1943 military strategy.

January 27. U.S. makes first bombings of Germany.

February 13. A women's unit is added to the U.S. Marine Corps.

March 2-4. Battle of the Bismarck Sea. American bombers sink a Japanese convoy of 22 ships, shooting down more than 50 Japanese planes.

April 18. Commander in chief of the Japanese navy, Admiral Yamamoto, is shot and killed in U.S. air raid.

April 23. U.S. and Britain set up headquarters in England to plan for the invasion of Europe.

May 7. Bizerte, Tunisia, is captured by American troops. The British take Tunis.

May 12. The North African campaign ends.

May 19. Winston Churchill addresses Congress.

May 30. U.S. retakes Attu, in the Aleutian Islands.

July 10. Allied forces invade Sicily.

July 19. 500 Allied planes bomb Rome.

July 24. Saturation bombing of Hamburg commences.

July 25. Benito Mussolini resigns, being overthrown by Pietro Badoglio.

August 11-24. Allies meet at the Quebec conference. Meetings include some Chinese representatives.

August 15. Canadian and American forces retake Kiska, in the Aleutians.

August 17. Allied forces conquer Sicily.

August 28. U.S. secures New Georgia, Solomon Islands.

September 3. Allied forces begin the invasion of Italy.

September 8. Unconditional surrender of Italy to the Allies. German forces and the small Nazi controlled Italian government continued to battle the Allies, occupying Italian strategic points, including Rome, for the next several months.

September 9. Allied landing at Salerno, Italy, including more than 700 American, British, Dutch, French, and Polish ships.

October 13. Italy declares war on Germany.

Below: Government posters such as this were displayed in public places all over America.

1778 1943

AMERICANS will _always_ fight for liberty

Above: 750 women volunteers lined up in Washington, D.C. on the first day of recruiting.

October 19. Moscow conference begins. British, American, Russian, and Chinese representatives agree on surrender terms for the enemy.

November 1. Landing of U.S. forces on Bougainville, Solomon Islands.

November 22. Roosevelt, Churchill, and Chiang Kai-Shek meet in Cairo, planning military strategy against Japan.

November 28-December 1. Roosevelt, Churchill, and Stalin meet in Teheran, planning a strategy for the Allied invasion of western Europe.

★★ 1944 ★★

January 16. General Eisenhower named supreme Commander of Allied Forces for the invasion of Europe.

January 22. The defeat of the German forces by the Allies continues on Italian soil, with the Allies establishing a beachhead at Anzio.

January 27. Germans are defeated by Soviets in Leningrad.

February 18. U.S. causes serious loss to Japanese forces in the Caroline Islands.

March 6. 800 U.S. Flying Fortresses bomb Berlin.

March 8. Japan begins a large scale offensive in Burma.

March 15. Japan invades India.

April 10. USSR recaptures Odessa.

April 22. U.S. forces invade New Guinea.

May 23. After 3 months on the beachhead at Anzio, Italy, the Allies take ground inland against the German army.

June 4. Allied forces enter Rome. American and British troops respect the holiday (Trinity Sunday), and do not occupy the city until the following morning.

June 6. Normandy invasion begins. Designated D-Day and code named Operation Overlord, invasion is commanded by Eisenhower. The operation involves more than 4000 ships, 3000 planes, and more than 4,000,000 Allied troops.

June 9. USSR attacks Finland.

June 15. U.S. bombs Tokyo.

June 19-20. U.S. defeats the Japanese fleet in the Battle of the Philippine Sea.

June 22. The Japanese are driven out of India.

June 27. Cherbourg, France is liberated by the Allies.

July 10. Saipan falls to U.S. forces.

July 21. U.S. invades Guam.

August 8. Brittany falls to Allies.

August 9. Guam falls to the U.S.

August 15. U.S. Seventh Army invades southern France.

August 21. Delegates from the U.S., Great Britain, China, and the U.S.S.R. meet at the Dumbarton Oaks conference in Washington, D.C., and lay the groundwork for the United Nations.

August 23. Rumania, part of the Axis, surrenders to the Soviets.

August 25. Paris is liberated by the Allies.

September 3. Brussels is liberated.

September 4. Antwerp is liberated.

September 8. Bulgaria, part of the Axis, joins the Allies and declares war on Germany.

September 12. U.S. First Army enters Germany.

September 17-27. British and American forces disastrously fail in the attempted invasion of the Netherlands.

September 19. Finland surrenders and signs armistice with the Allies.

Left: A battalion of African-American soldiers practices an abandon ship drill. The races were not integrated while serving in the armed forces.

October 2. Poland continues to be fought for by Germans and Soviets. Germans crush a Polish revolt.

October 14. British take Athens. The German general Rommel, head of German forces in that city, commits suicide.

October 20. MacArthur and American forces return to the Philippines. Soviets take Belgrade, the key battle in the defeat of Yugoslavia.

October 21. After 2 days of house-to-house fighting, Aachen, Germany, falls to Allied forces.

October 23-26. Battle of Leyte Gulf. The Japanese suffer heavy losses in the largest naval battle of the war.

November 7. FDR is elected President for an unprecedented fourth term. Harry S. Truman is elected Vice-President.

December 16. Battle of the Bulge begins. Final major German offensive of the war brings only temporary success. By mid-January, all ground taken in the German offensive is retaken by the Allies.

★★ 1945 ★★

January 16. German forces defeated by the Allies as the Battle of the Bulge concludes.

January 17. Warsaw is taken by the Soviets as Germans retreat from the eastern front.

January 20. Hungary signs armistice with the Allies.

February 4-11. Roosevelt, Churchill, and Stalin meet at the Yalta conference to deal with the postwar reorganization of Europe.

February 7. General MacArthur, with the U.S. Sixth Army, returns to Manila more than three years after being forced out by the Japanese.

February 8. Allies begin the push to the Rhine River.

February 13. Participants in the Yalta Conference call for a United Nations Conference. Allied bombings destroy most of the German city of Dresden.

March 3. U.S. liberates Manila from Japanese occupation.

March 7. U.S. First Army crosses the Remagen Bridge over the Rhine River into Germany.

March 16. After 36 days of fighting Iwo Jima falls to the U.S. Marines.

March 22-23. General Patton and his troops cross the Rhine at Oppenheim. General Montgomery crosses the Rhine just north of Ruhr.

April 1. U.S. forces invade Okinawa.

April 7. Soviets enter Vienna.

April 12. President Franklin Delano Roosevelt dies in Warm Springs, Georgia. Vice-President Harry S. Truman takes the oath of office.

April 16. Soviets begin the attack of Berlin.

April 23. Soviets enter Berlin.

April 24. Delegates from 50 nations attend the United Nations conference at San Francisco.

April 28. Benito Mussolini and his mistress are abducted and shot. Their disfigured bodies were strung up and spat upon in the streets of Milan.

April 29. German army in Italy surrenders to the Allies. Americans liberate 32,000 prisoners at the Dachau concentration camp.

April 30. Adolf Hitler and Eva Braun commit suicide in Berlin. They had been married the day before. Allied forces take Munich.

May 3. German army in Berlin surrenders to the Russians.

May 7. Germany surrenders unconditionally to Allied forces.

May 8. V-E Day. The European facet of the war ends with ratification of the German surrender agreement in Berlin.

June 5. Germany is divided into 4 occupation zones by the Allies, the primary powers being U.S., USSR, British, and French.

June 21. Okinawa falls to U.S. forces.

July 5. MacArthur declares the Philippine Islands liberated.

July 16. U.S. detonates the first atomic bomb near Alamogardo, New Mexico.

July 17-August 2. At Potsdam, Churchill, Truman and Stalin meet to plan the final assault on the Japanese and the peace agreements in Europe.

July 26. Churchill is no longer Prime Minister of Britain, replaced by Clement Attlee.

July 28. U.S. Senate ratifies the United Nations Charter.

August 6. U.S. destroys Hiroshima, Japan, with the first atomic bomb to be used in war.

August 9. Nagasaki, Japan is destroyed as the U.S. drops the second and, to date, last atomic weapon to be used in war.

August 14. Japan surrenders unconditionally to Allied Forces.

August 15. V-J Day. Americans receive word that World War II is officially over.

September 2. Formal surrender ceremonies on USS Missouri.

Far Left: *WAAC officer candidates in class at Fort Des Moines, Iowa.*

Left: *An actual ration book.*

A WORLD SHAPED BY WAR
The Aftermath

November 20, 1945. Nuremberg War Trials begin, revealing to the world the horror of the holocaust.

January 7, 1946. United Nations opens its first session in London.

July 4, 1946. The Philippines declare independence.

September 15, 1946. Continuing the spread of the Soviet sphere, a Communist government takes over the rule of Bulgaria.

November 20-23, 1946. The ruling French army attacks the rebel Communist army at Haiphong, Vietnam.

January 12, 1947. A Soviet-backed Communist government is established in Poland.

February 10, 1947. The non-German Axis nations, Bulgaria, Italy, Rumania, Hungary, and Finland, formally sign a peace treaty.

June 5, 1947. The Marshall Plan is put into effect.

August 14, 1947. India and Pakistan declare their independence from Great Britain.

December 30, 1947. Communists come to power in Rumania.

January 4, 1948. Burma declares its independence.

April 1, 1948. Soviets blockade Berlin, which is part of their quadrant in the Marshall Plan. The U.S. airlifts food and supplies into the city.

May 14, 1948. The State of Israel is officially begun as a country.

June 14, 1948. Soviet Communists come to power in Czechoslovakia.

April 4, 1949. NATO, the North Atlantic Treaty Organization, is formed as a response of western Allies to the Soviet threat.

May 12, 1949. The Berlin blockade is ended by Soviets.

May 15, 1949. Communists come to power in Hungary.

May 23, 1949. A divided Germany is made official as West Germany becomes a separate country, with the Soviet controlled East Germany partitioned off as a territory unto itself.

September 24, 1949. The Soviets successfully test an atomic bomb.

October 1, 1949. The civil war in China ends with the declaration of the People's Republic of China.

October 7, 1949. East Germany officially is called the German Democratic Republic.

October 16, 1949. The civil war in Greece ends after 5 years of fighting.

June 25, 1949. The Korean War begins with North Korea's attack of South Korea.

September 8, 1951. Japan signs an official peace treaty in San Francisco.

April 28, 1952. The occupying American troops make their final withdrawal from Japan.

July 27, 1953. Korean War ends.

May 8, 1954. After 8 years of fighting, French forces are defeated at Dienbienphu, Vietnam.

July 21, 1954. Vietnam is officially partitioned into North and South.

In November of 1989 the Berlin Wall fell, and the re-unification of Germany began. Also in that year and the next, the Soviet control of eastern Europe unraveled. Those countries annexed to the Soviet sphere as a result of World War II were largely peacefully restored to self-rule. The Union of Soviet Socialist Republics, the empire largely empowered by the Soviet role in World War II, was officially dissolved.

Left: In New York smokers line up to buy rationed cigarettes.

O'ER THE RAMPARTS WE WATCH

Ac-cent-tchu-ate The Positive

from the Motion Picture HERE COME THE WAVES

Registration 7
Rhythm: Swing

Lyric by Johnny Mercer
Music by Harold Arlen

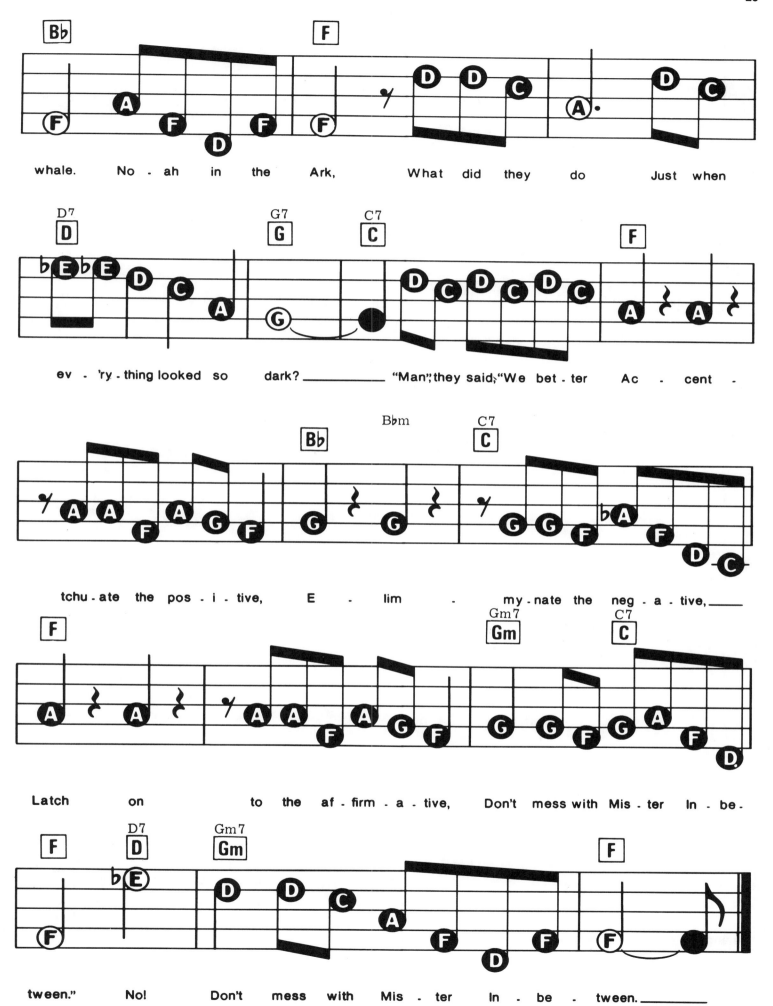

The Anniversary Waltz

Registration 3
Rhythm: Waltz

Words and Music by Al Dubin
and Dave Franklin

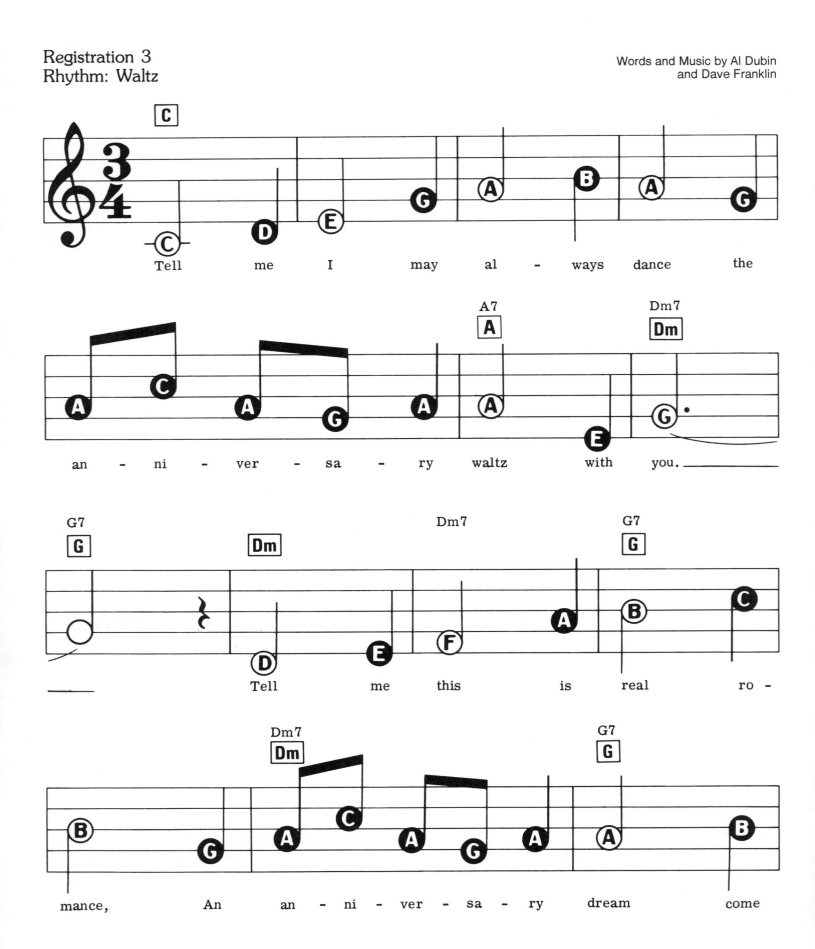

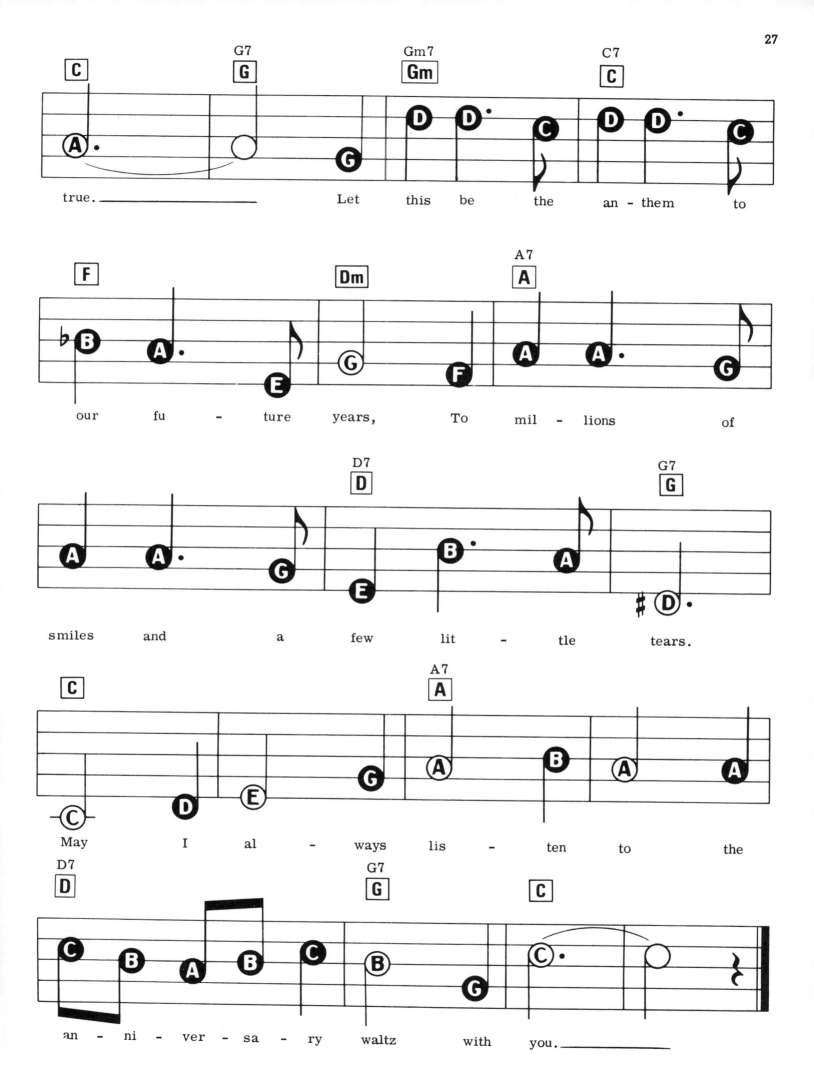

Be Careful, It's My Heart
from *HOLIDAY INN*

Registration 1
Rhythm: Swing

Words and Music by
Irving Berlin

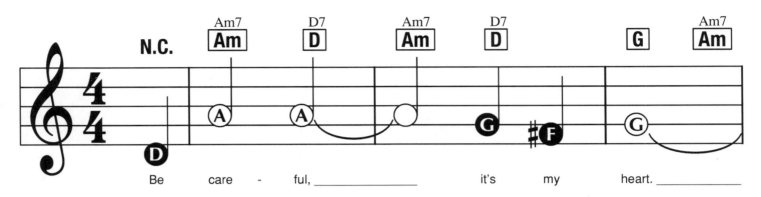

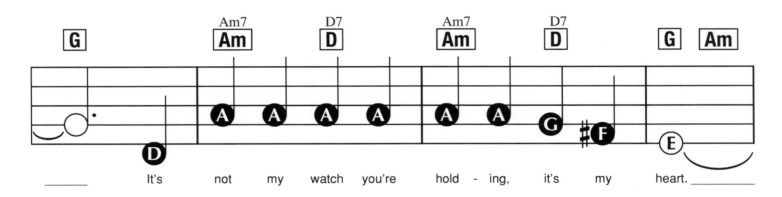

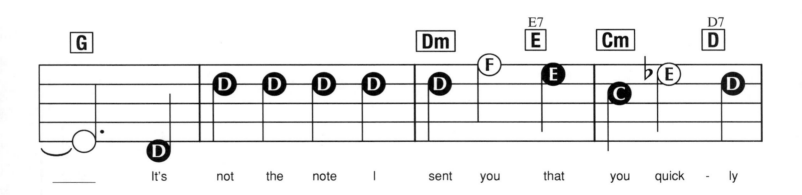

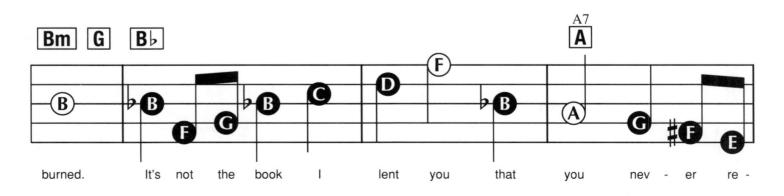

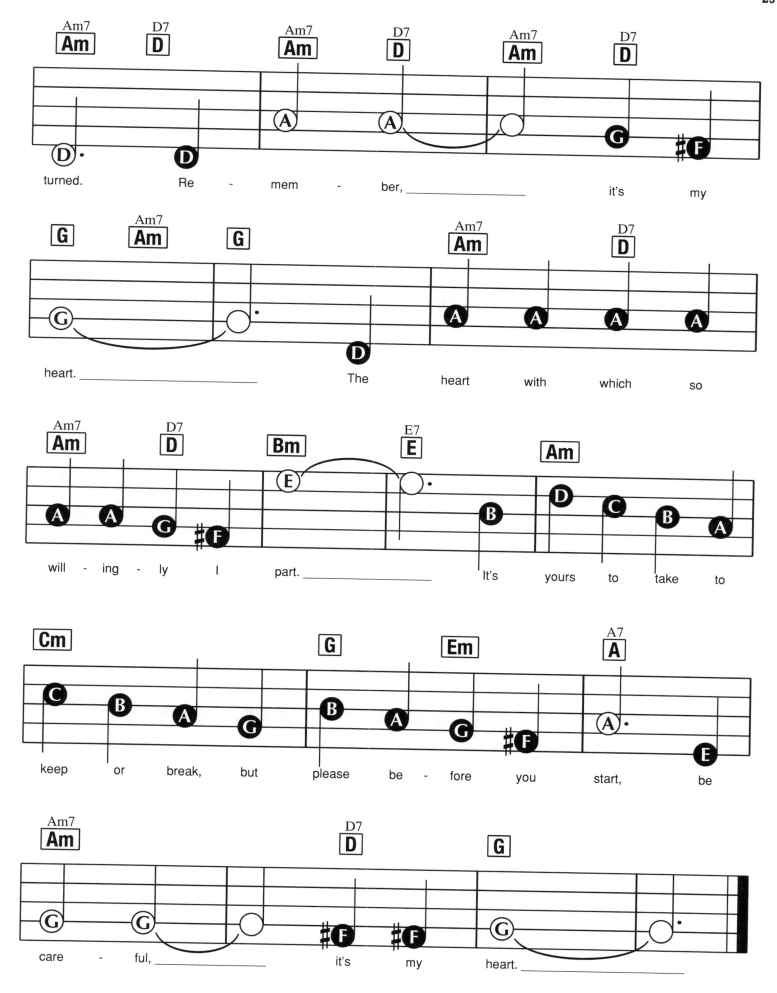

Boogie Woogie Bugle Boy

Registration 7
Rhythm: Shuffle or Fox Trot

Words and Music by Don Raye
and Hughie Prince

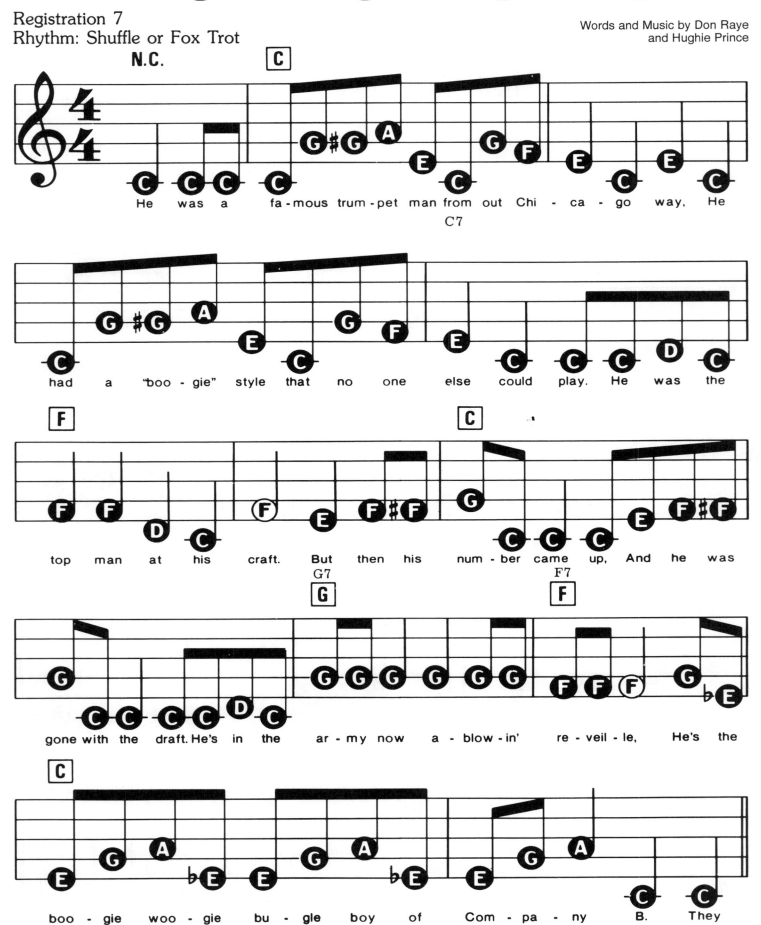

MCA music publishing

31

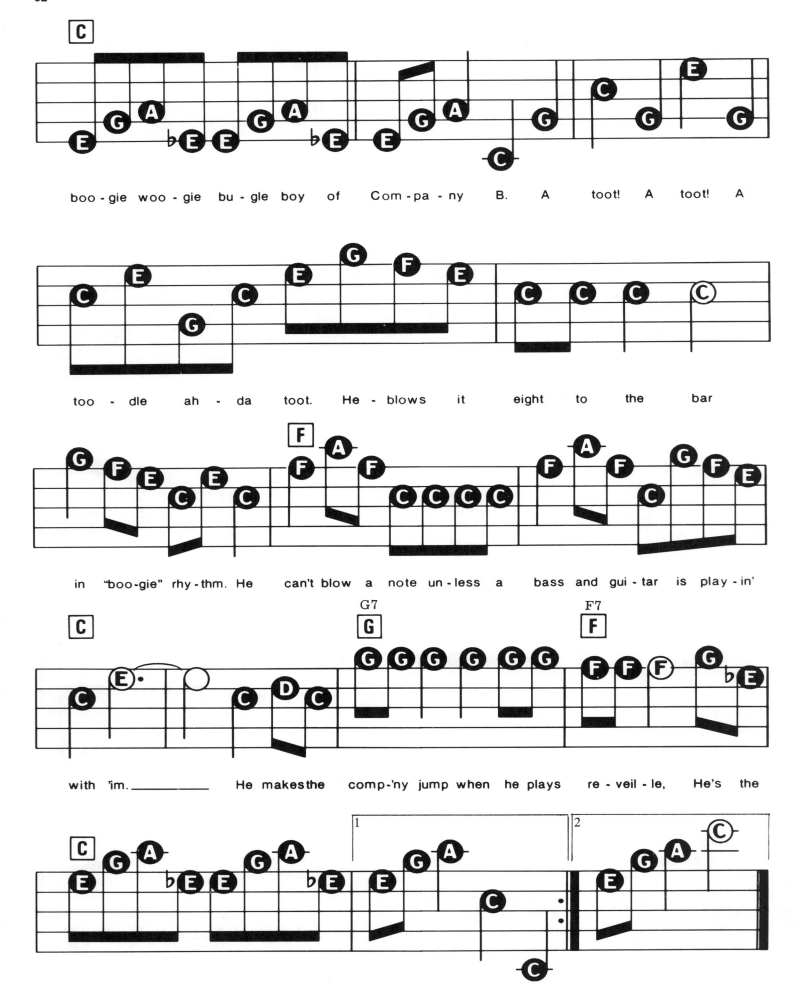

Don't Get Around Much Anymore

Registration 5
Rhythm: Fox Trot or Swing

Words and Music by Bob Russell
and Duke Ellington

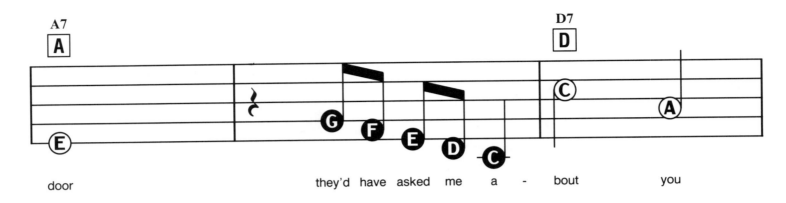

door   they'd have asked me a - bout you

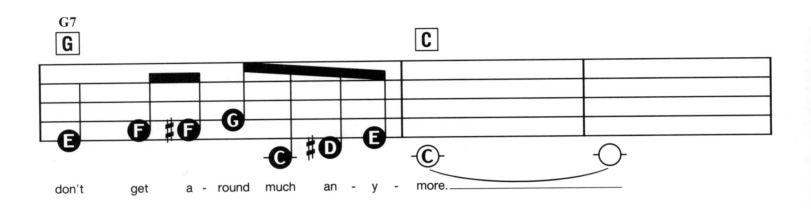

don't get a - round much an - y - more.___

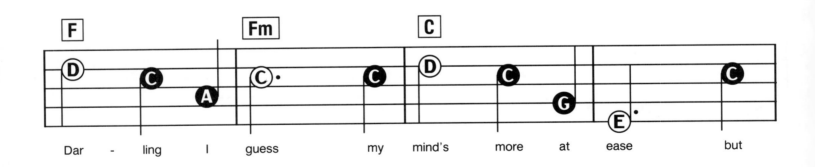

Dar - ling I guess my mind's more at ease but

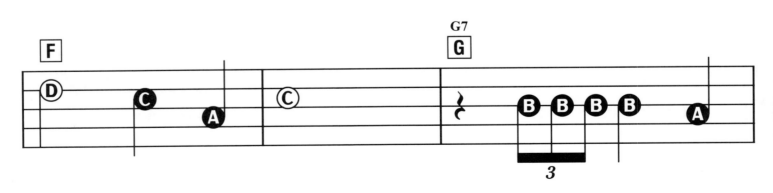

nev - er - the - less   why stir up mem - o -

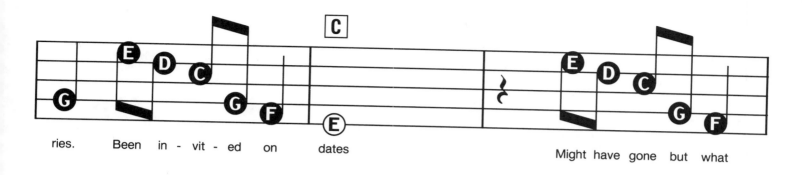

ries. Been in-vit-ed on dates

Might have gone but what

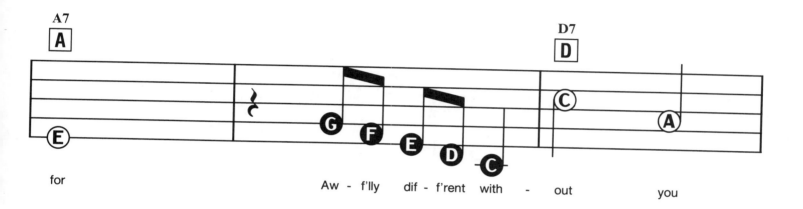

for

Aw-f'lly dif-f'rent with-out you

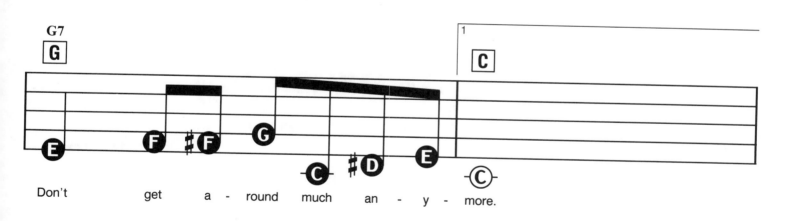

Don't get a-round much an-y-more.

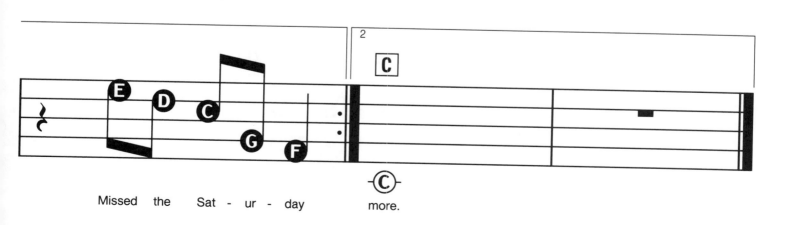

Missed the Sat-ur-day more.

Do Nothin' Till You Hear From Me

Registration 7
Rhythm: Swing

Words and Music by Bob Russell
and Duke Ellington

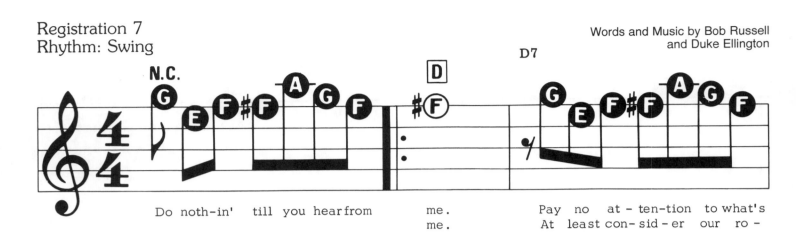

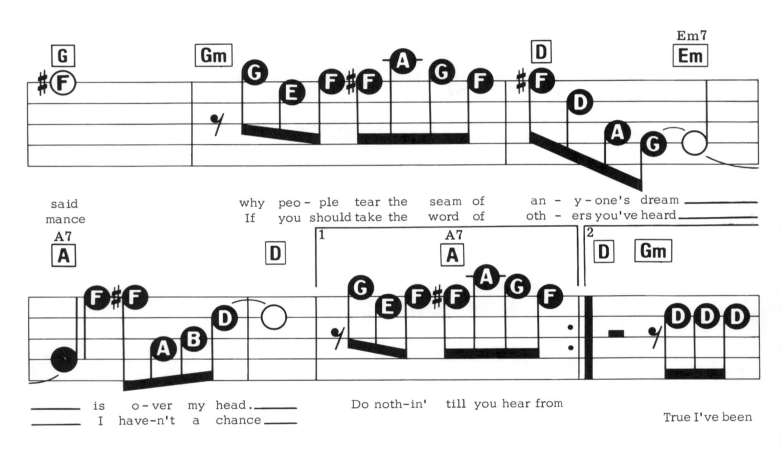

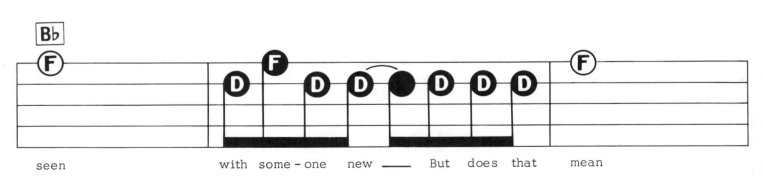

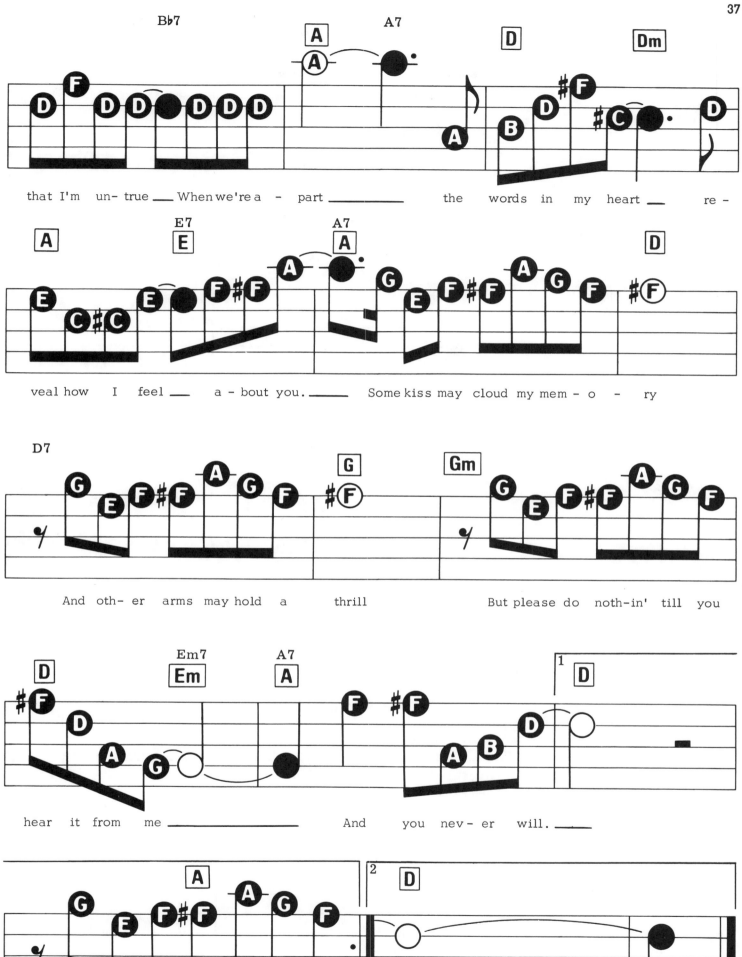

that I'm un-true ___ When we're a - part _____ the words in my heart ___ re -

veal how I feel ___ a - bout you. _____ Some kiss may cloud my mem - o - ry

And oth- er arms may hold a thrill But please do noth-in' till you

hear it from me _____ And you nev - er will. ____

Do noth-in' till you hear from

Don't Sit Under The Apple Tree
(With Anyone Else But Me)

Registration 2
Rhythm: Polka or Fox Trot

Words and Music by Lew Brown,
Sam H. Stept and Charlie Tobias

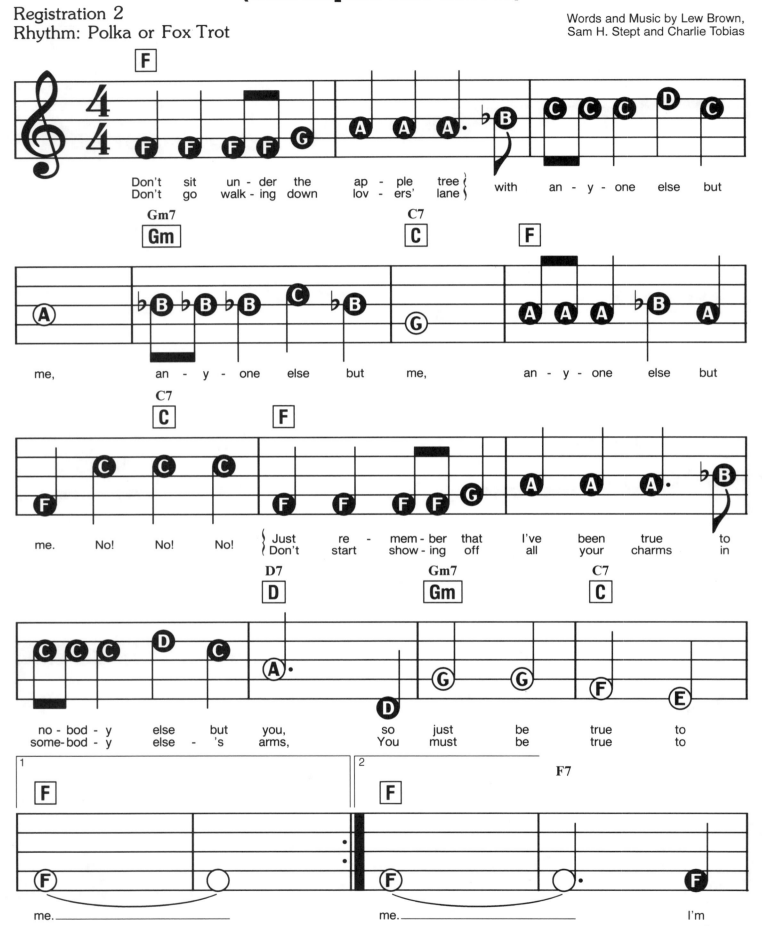

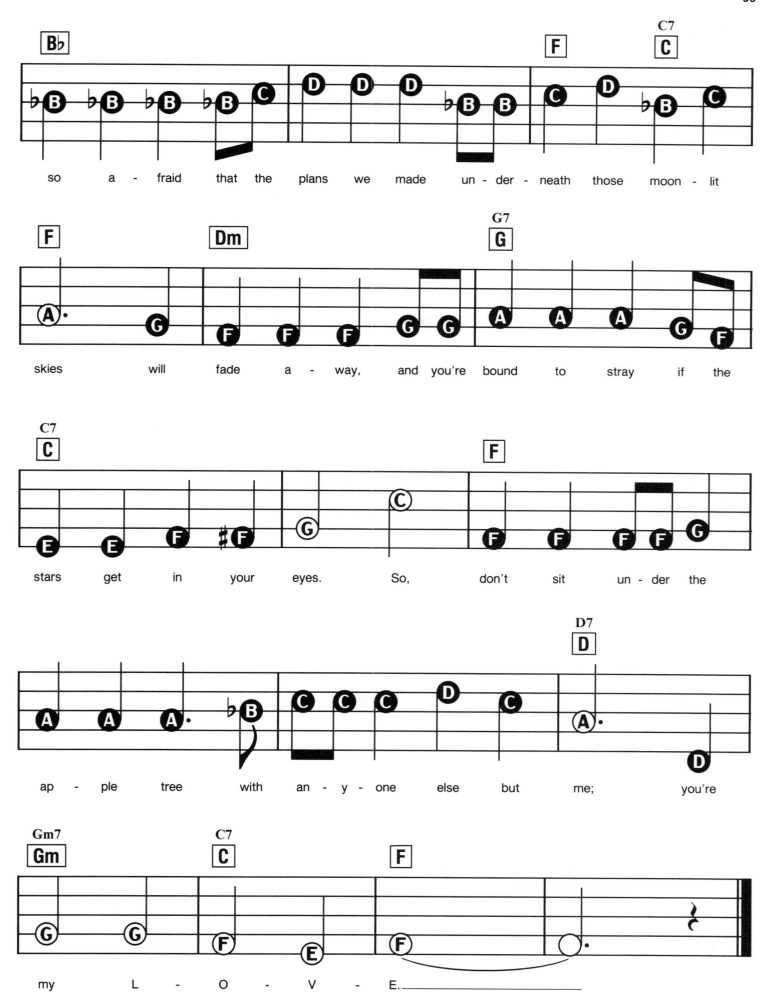

Ev'ry Time We Say Goodbye
from SEVEN LIVELY ARTS

Registration 1
Rhythm: Latin or Bossa Nova

Words and Music by
Cole Porter

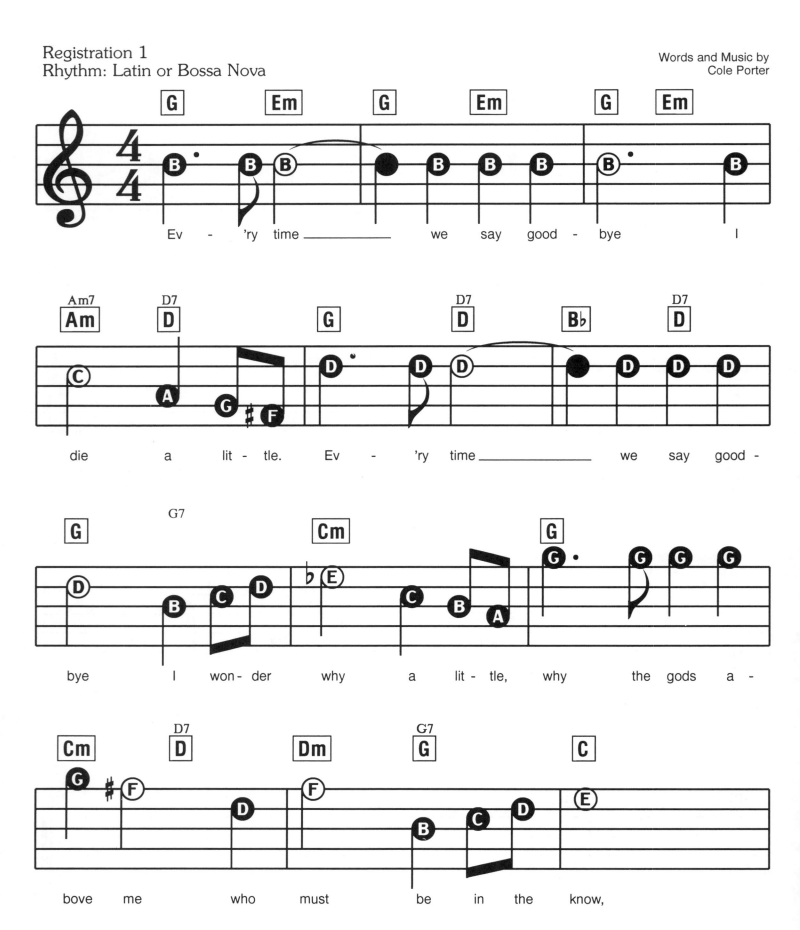

41

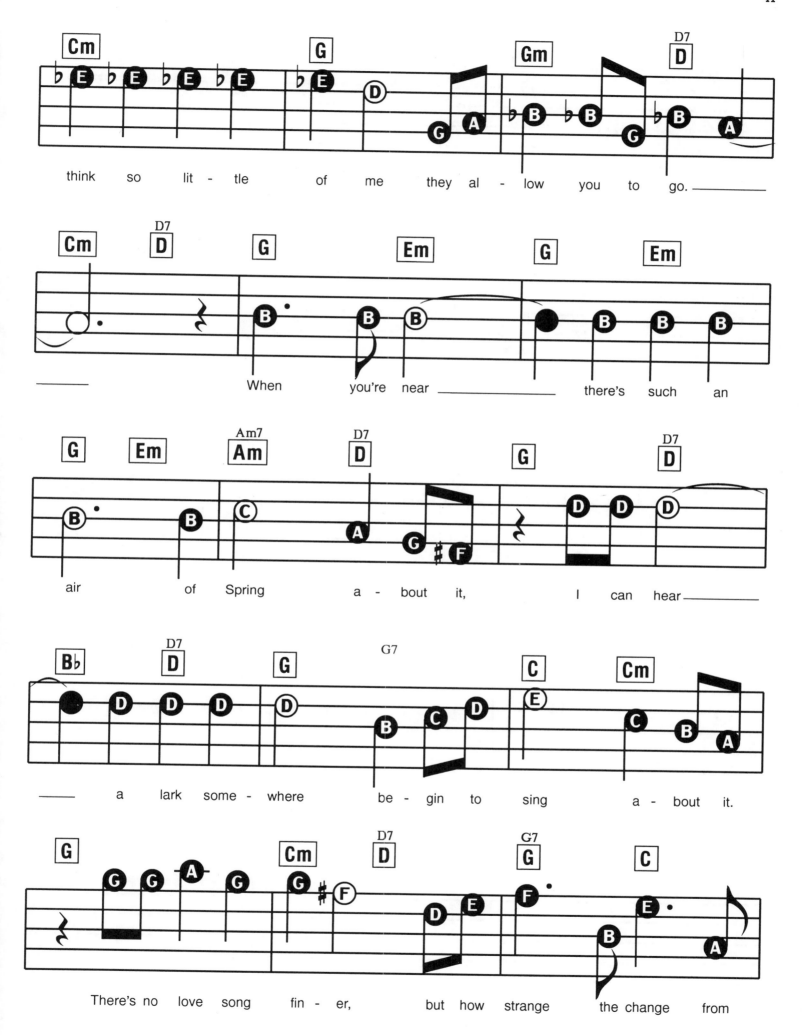

42

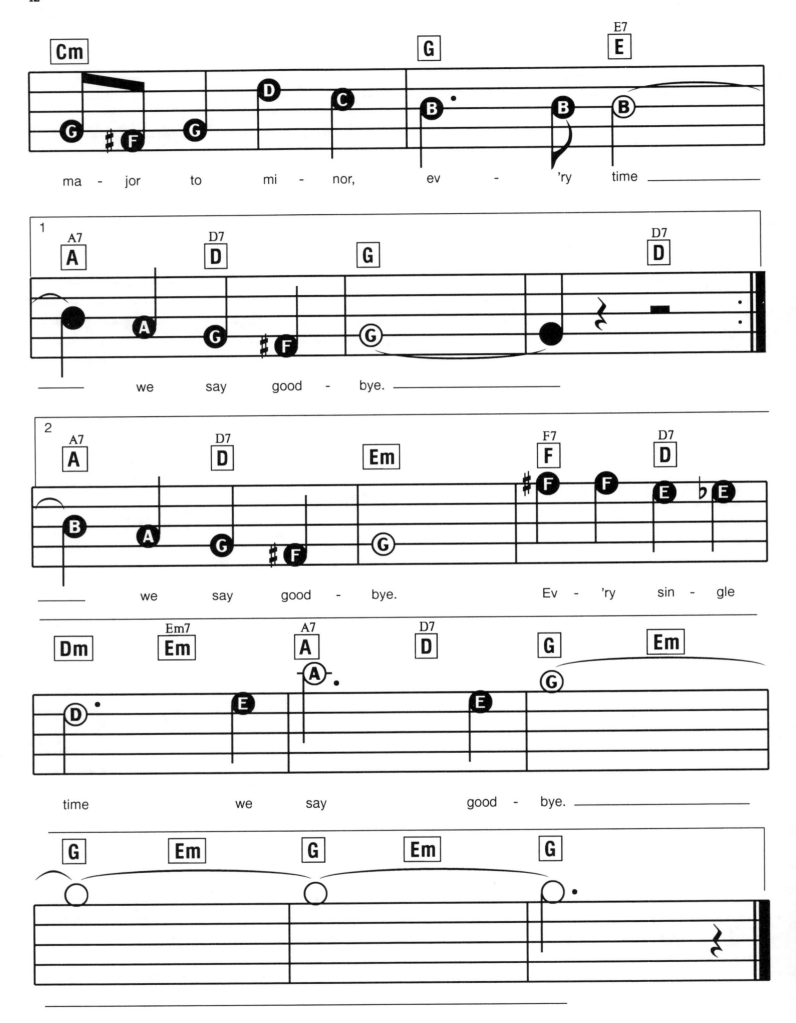

Have I Stayed Away Too Long

Registration 2
Rhythm: Fox Trot or Swing

By Frank Loesser

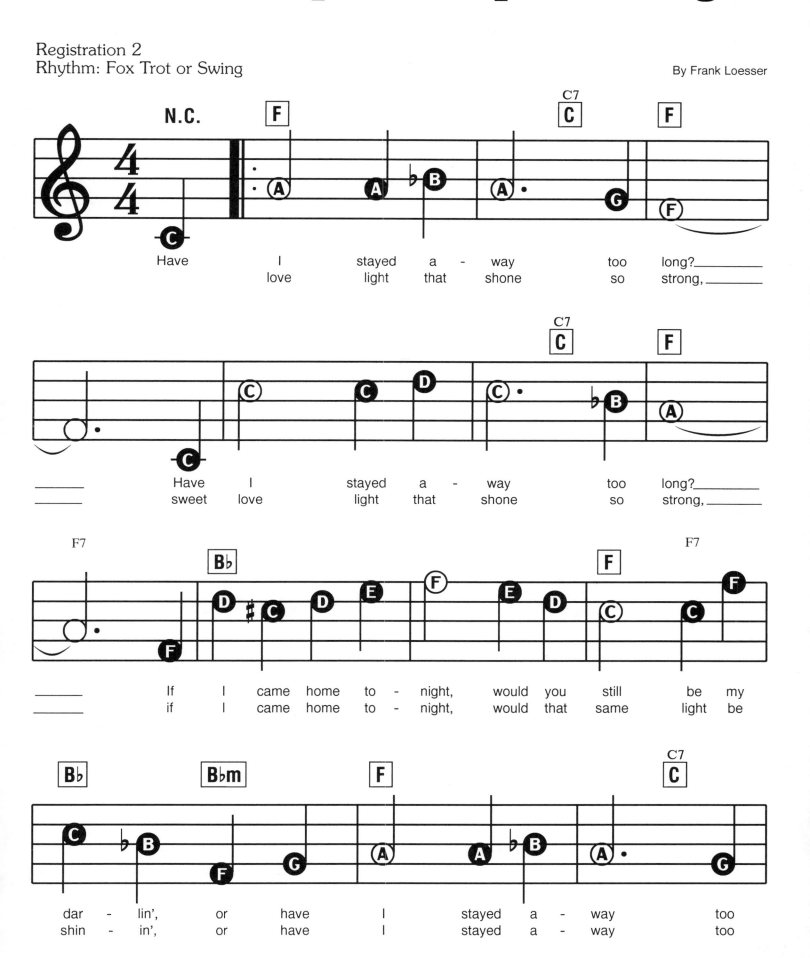

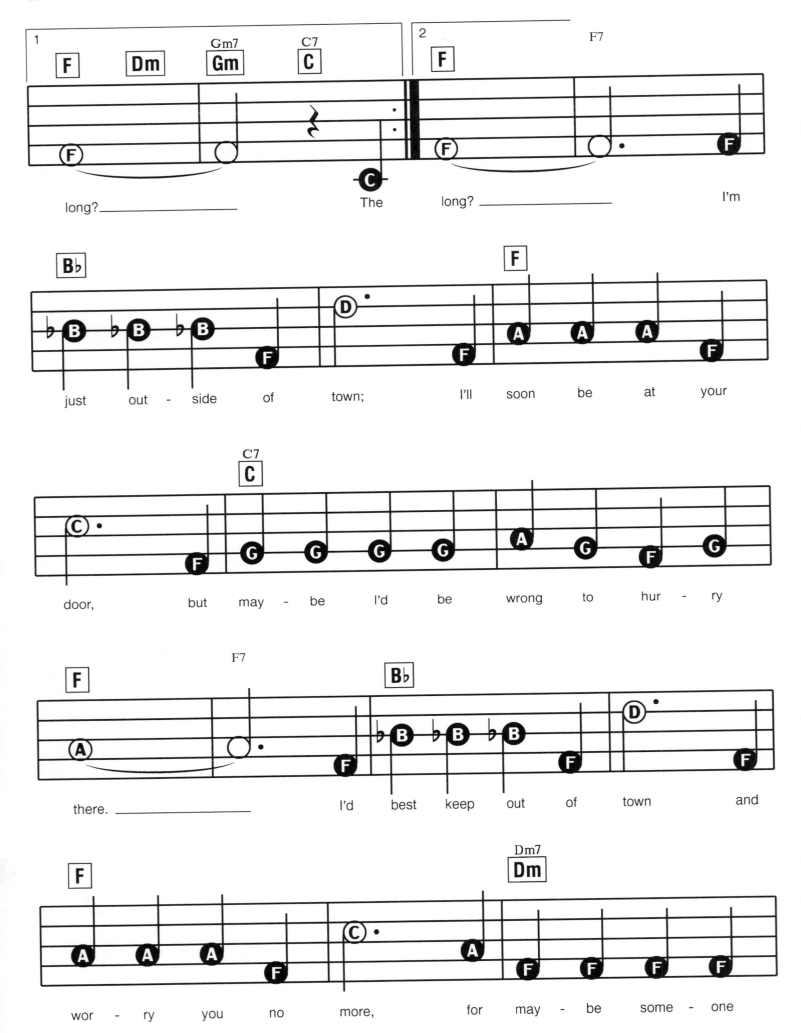

44

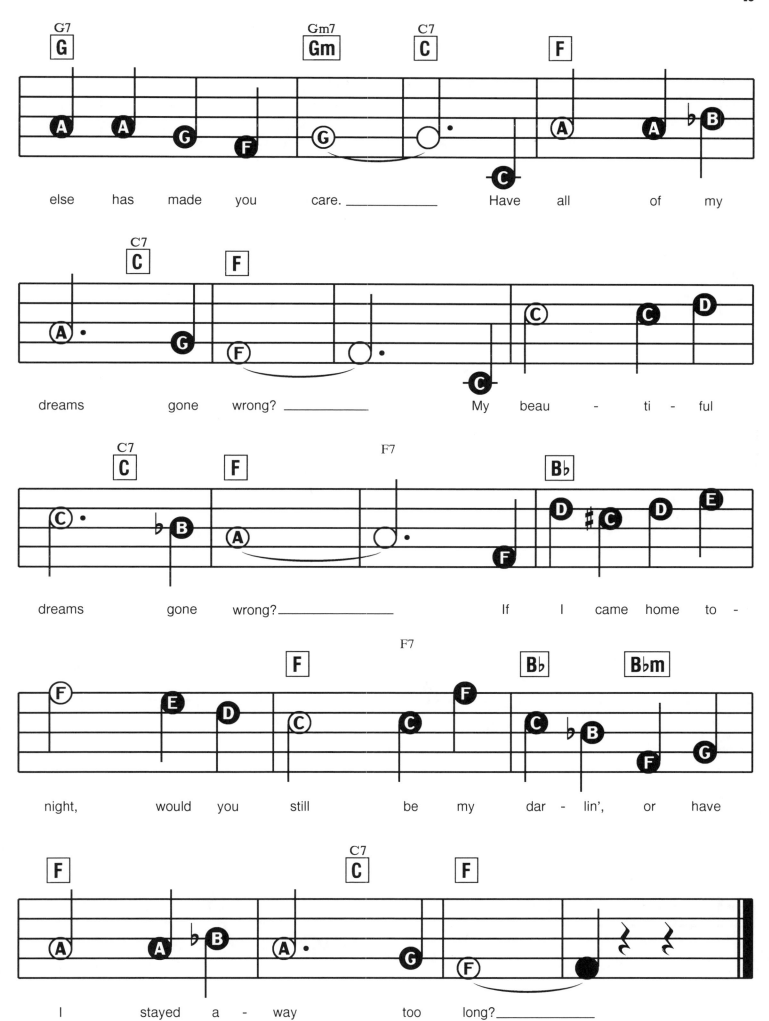

The Fleet's In

from THE FLEET'S IN

Registration 5
Rhythm: Fox Trot or Swing

Words by Johnny Mercer
Music by Victor Schertzinger

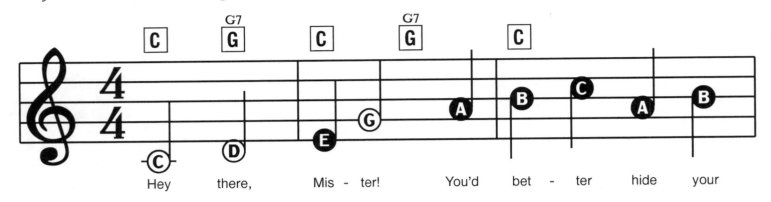

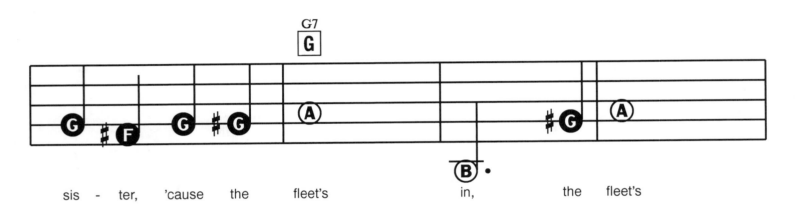

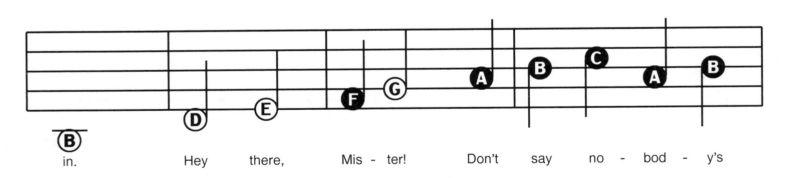

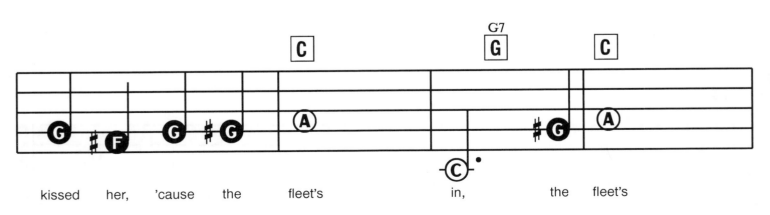

47

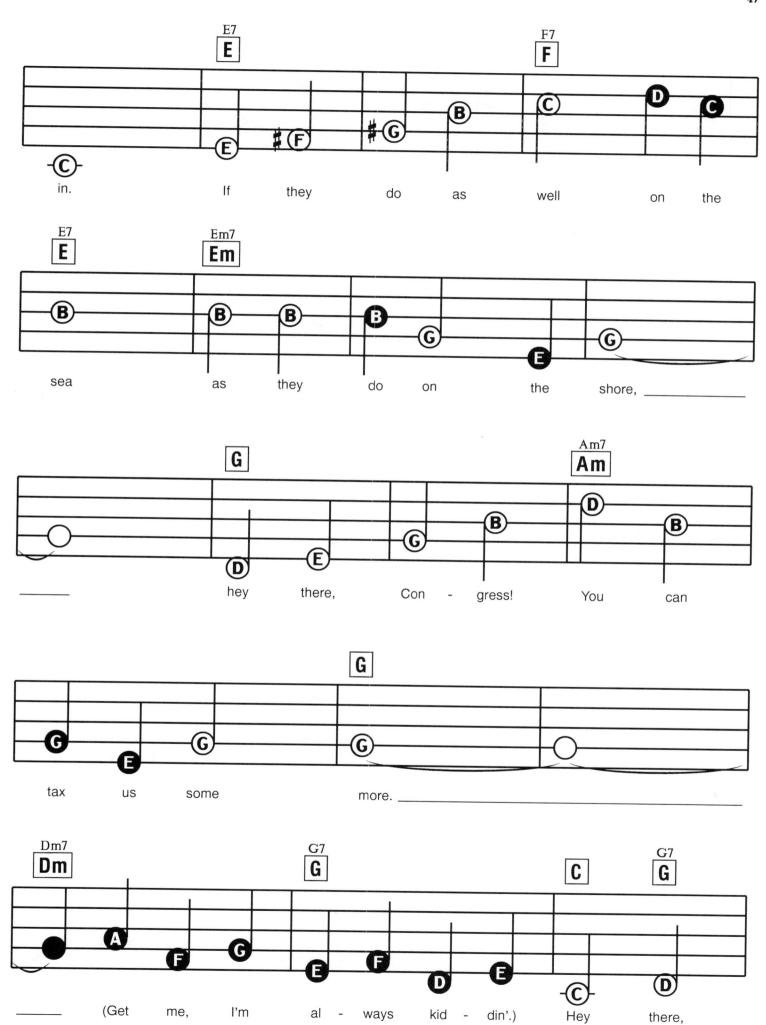

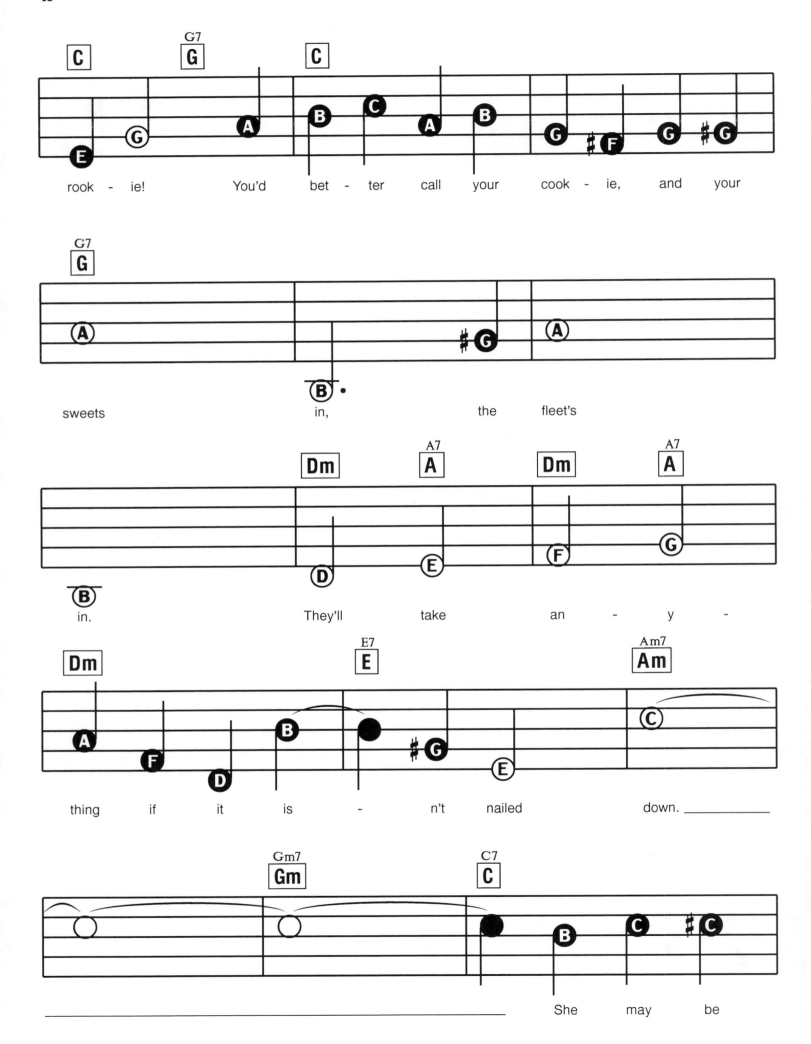

dark   or   fair,   those   sail - ors   don't   care _____

_____   as   long   as   she's   wear - ing   a

gown. _____   So   if   you   love her,   keep

un - der - cov - er the   fleet's   in

town. _____   town. _____

I Came Here To Talk For Joe

Registration 6
Rhythm: Fox Trot or Ballad

Words and Music by Lew Brown,
Charlie Tobias and Sam Stept

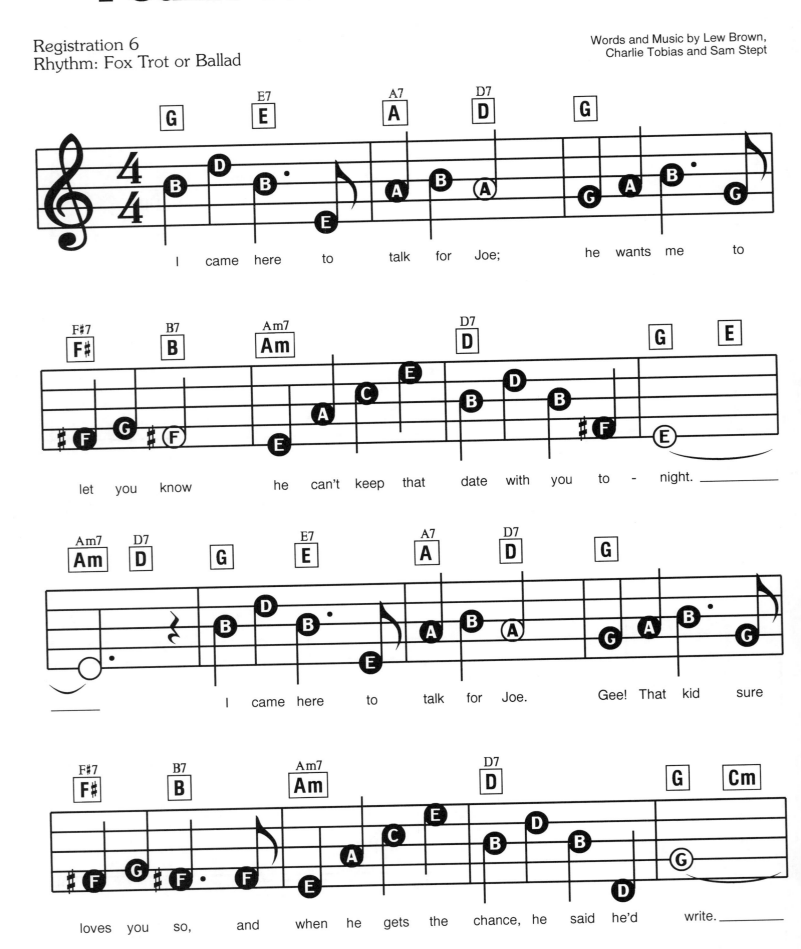

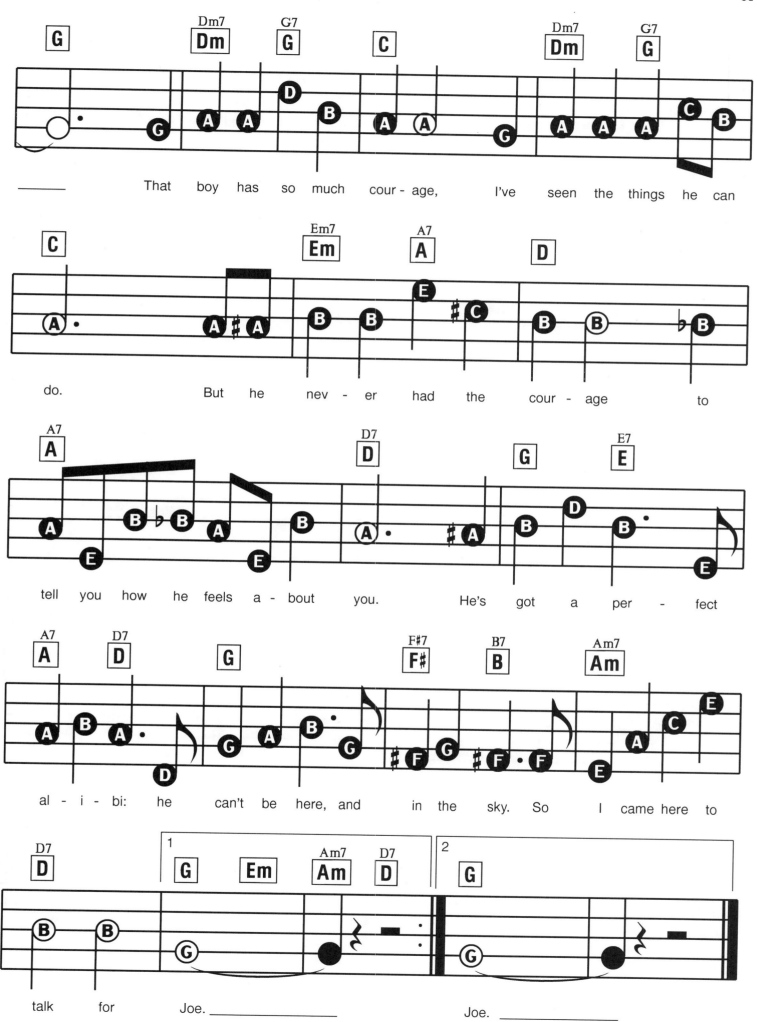

I Don't Want To Set
The World On Fire

Registration 5
Rhythm: Fox Trot

Words and Music by Sol Marcus,
Bennie Benjamin and Eddie Seiler

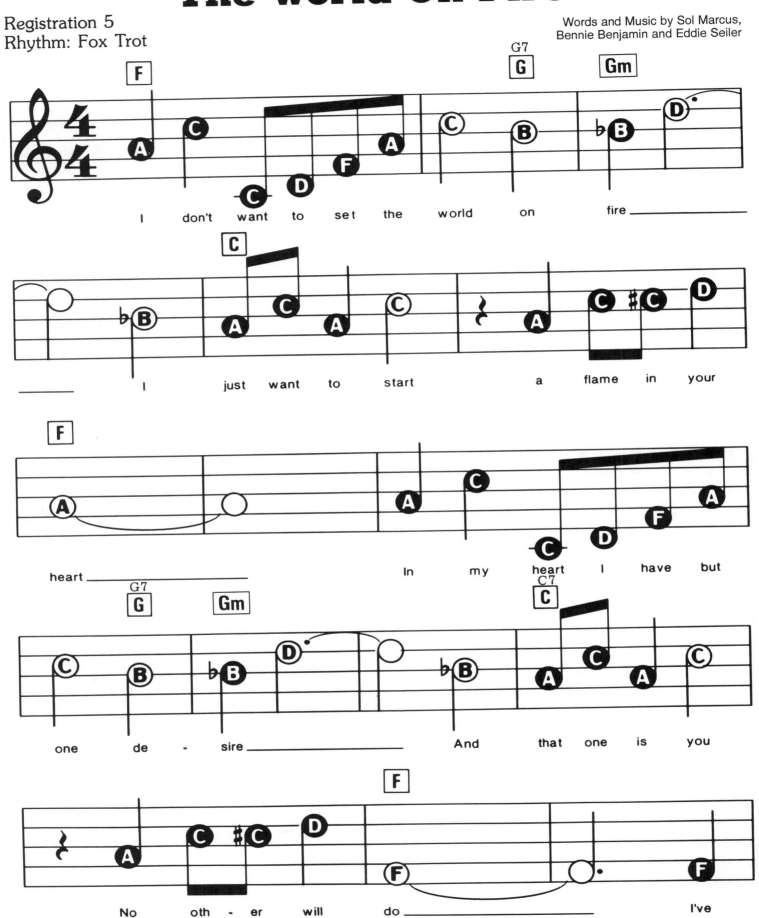

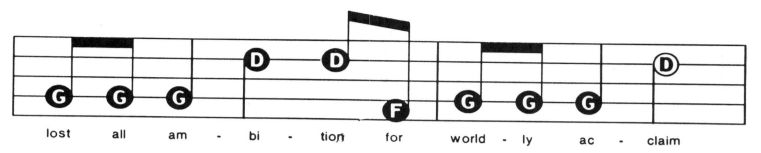

F7

lost all am - bi - tion for world - ly ac - claim

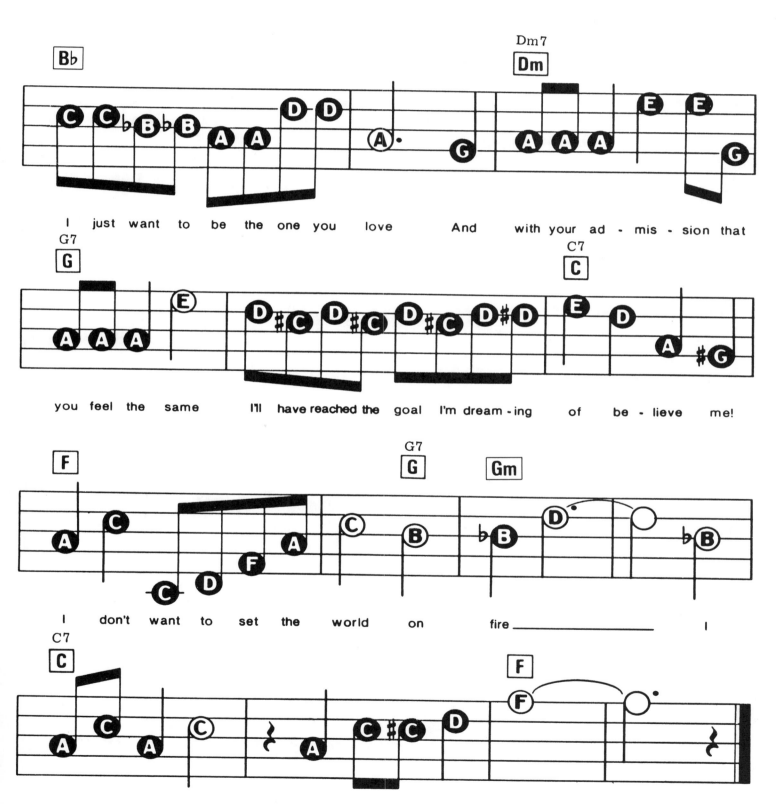

I just want to be the one you love   And   with your ad - mis - sion that

you feel the same   I'll have reached the goal I'm dream - ing   of   be - lieve me!

I   don't want to set the world   on   fire _____   I

just want to start   a flame in your   heart _____

I Don't Want To Walk Without You

from the Paramount Picture SWEATER GIRL

Registration 1
Rhythm: Swing

Words by Frank Loesser
Music by Jule Styne

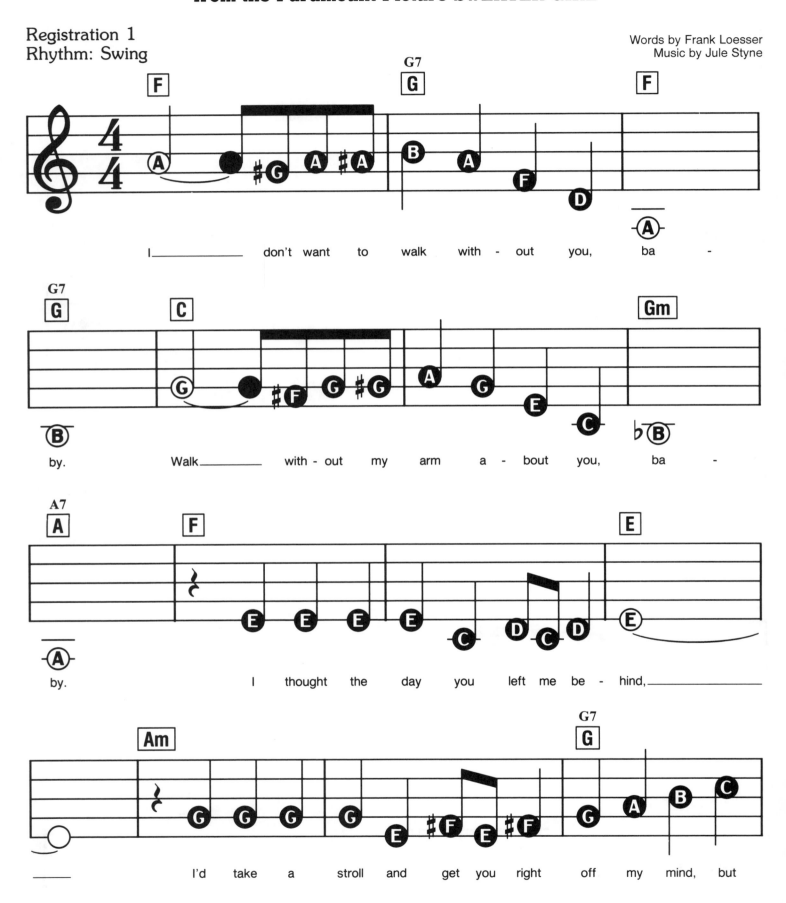

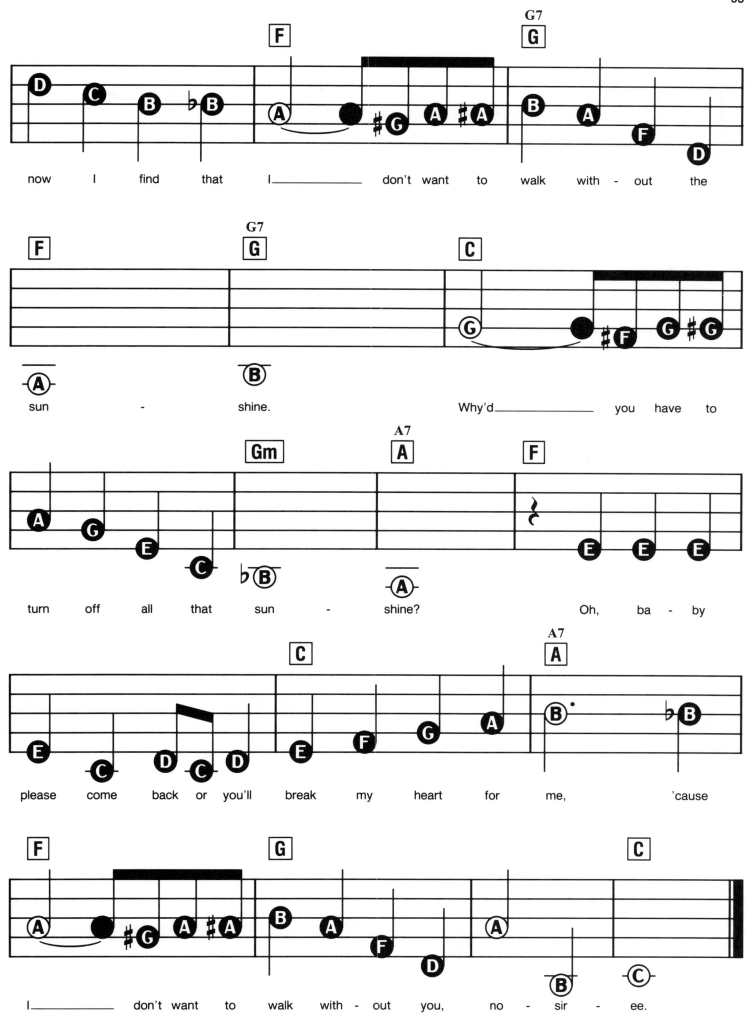

I'll Be Home For Christmas

Registration 1
Rhythm: Fox Trot or Swing

Words and Music by Kim Gannon
and Walter Kent

Introduction: 4 Measures

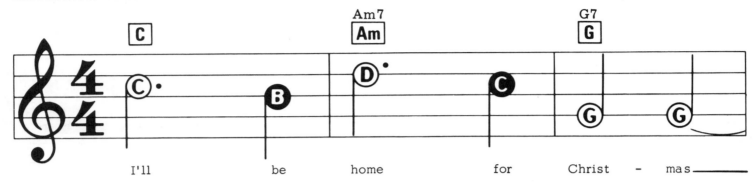

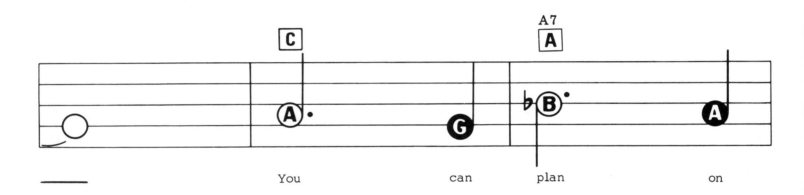

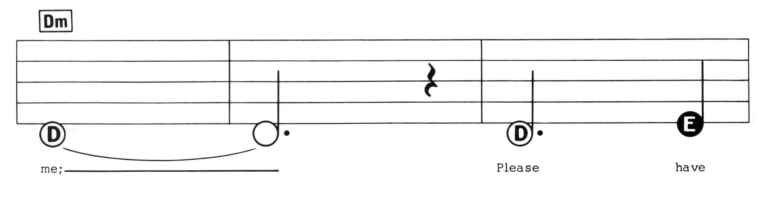

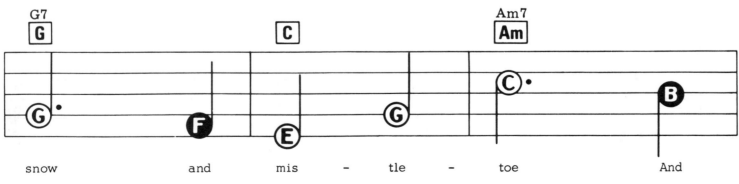

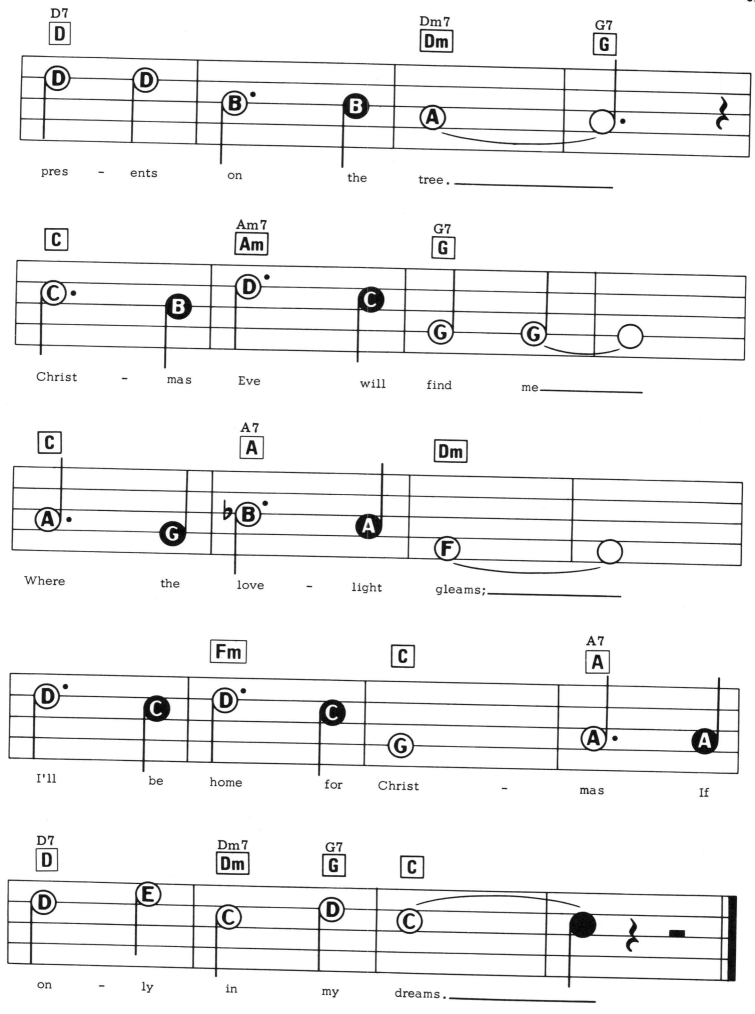

I'll Be Seeing You
from RIGHT THIS WAY

Lyric by Irving Kahal
Music by Sammy Fain

Registration 5
Rhythm: Swing

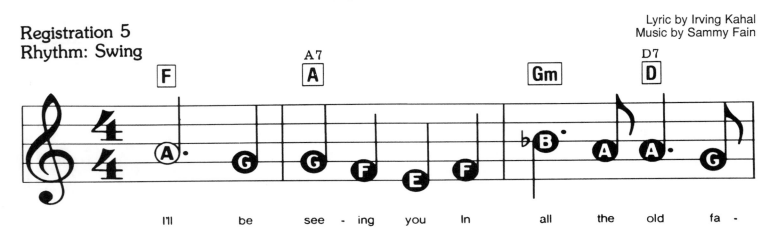

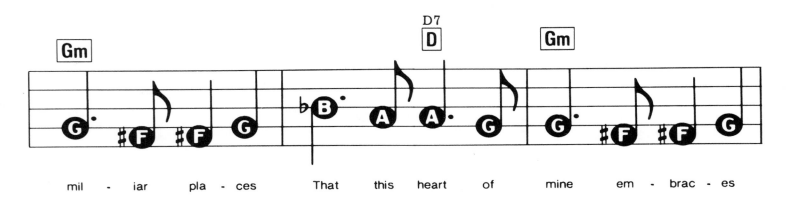

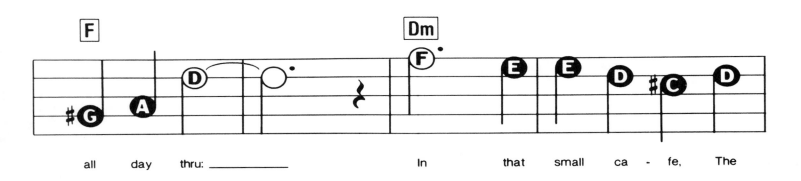

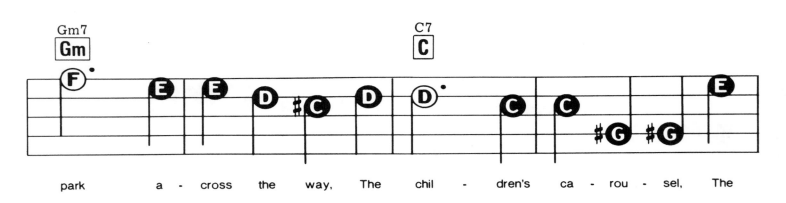

59

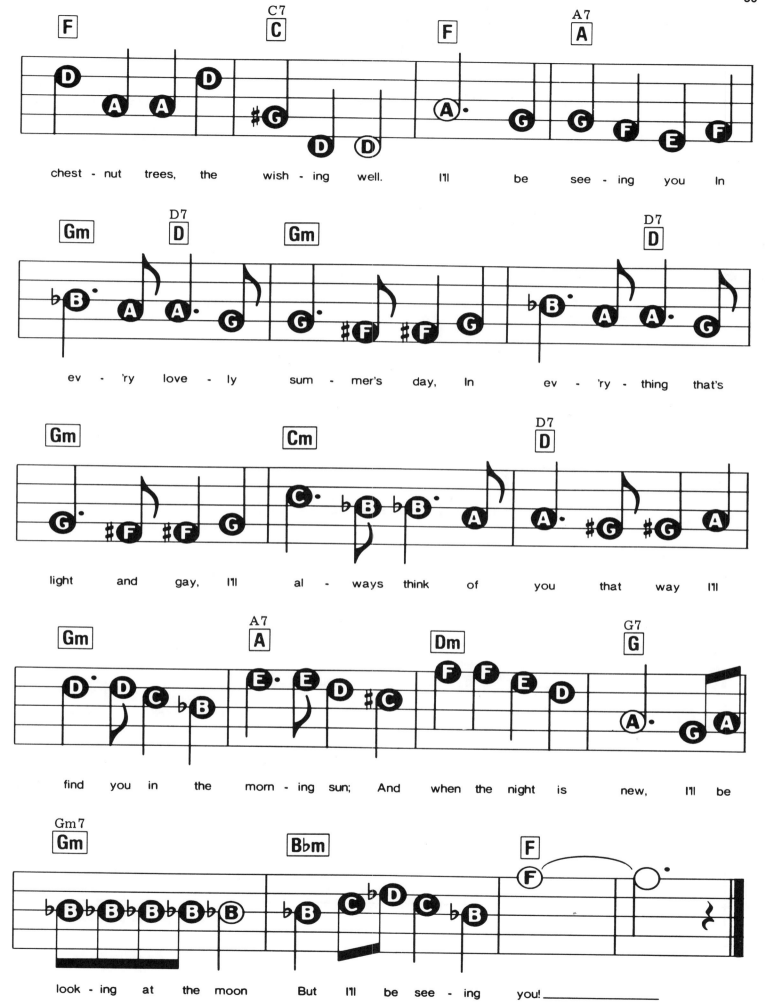

I'll Get By
(As Long As I Have You)

Registration 2
Rhythm: Fox Trot or Swing

Lyric by Roy Turk
Music by Fred E. Ahlert

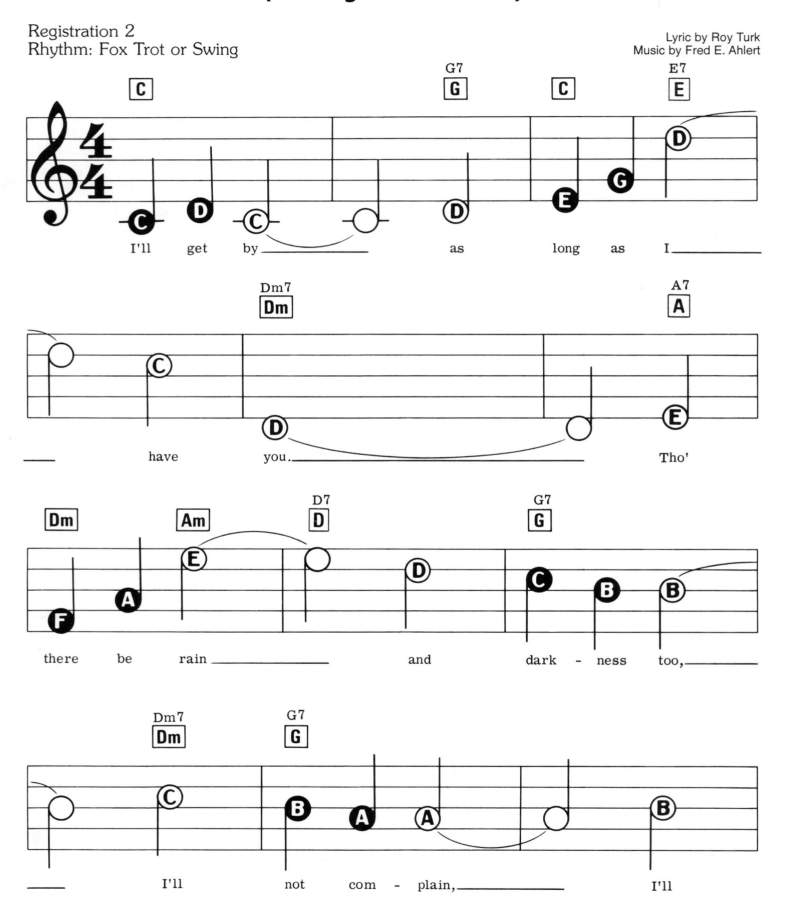

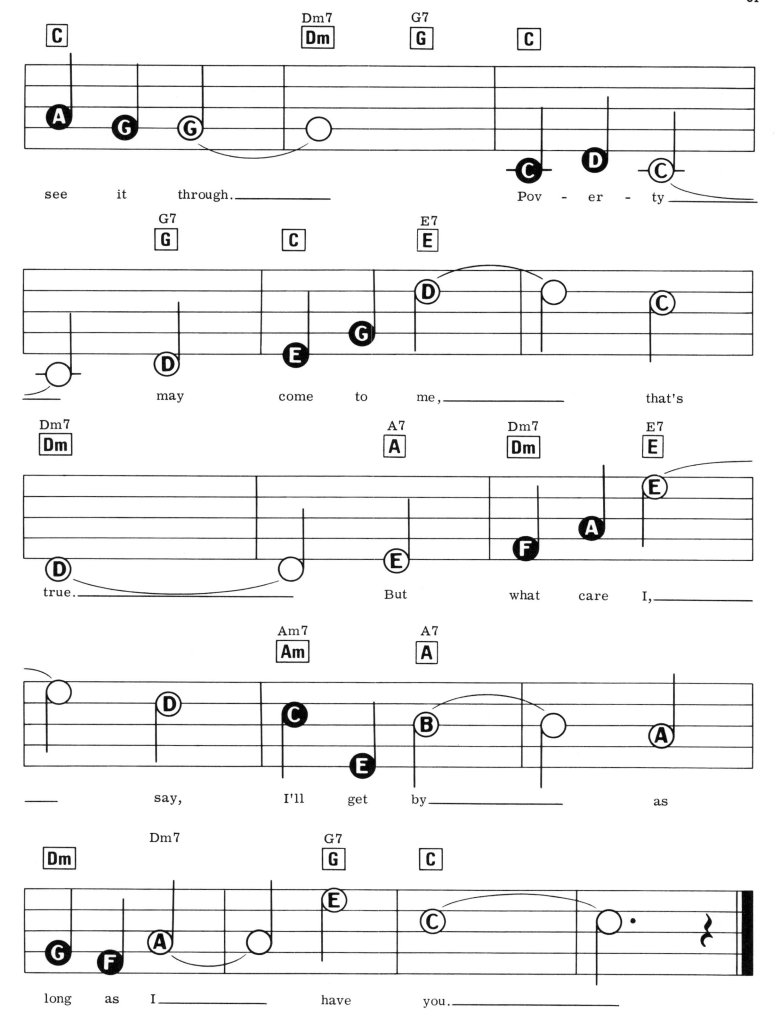

I'll Never Smile Again

Registration 9
Rhythm: Swing or Fox Trot

Words and Music by
Ruth Lowe

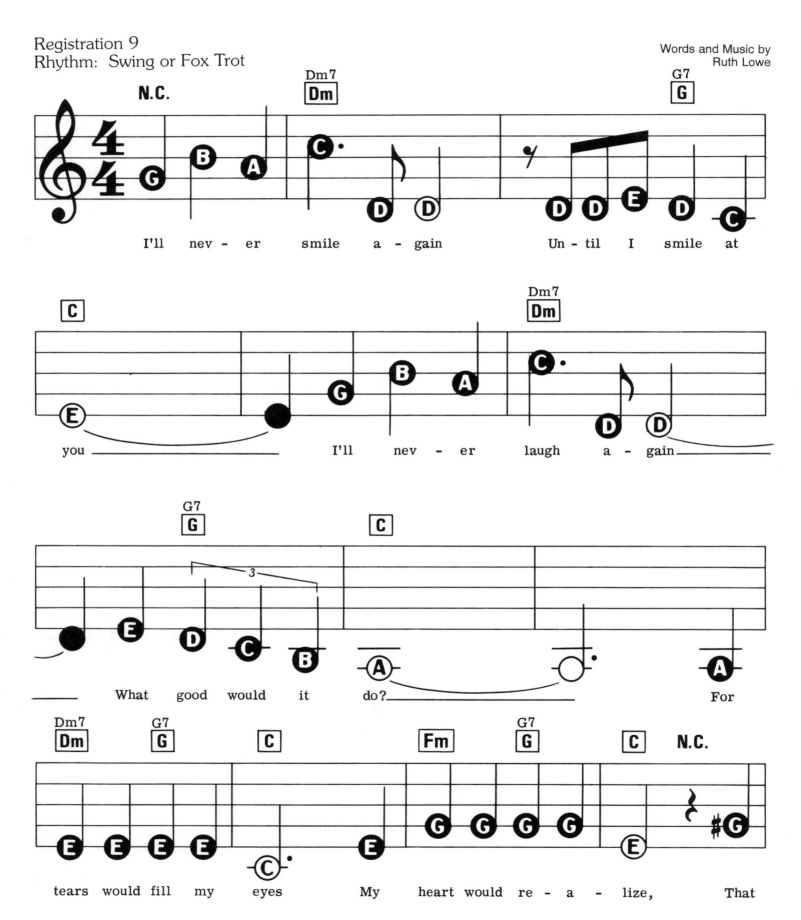

MCA music publishing

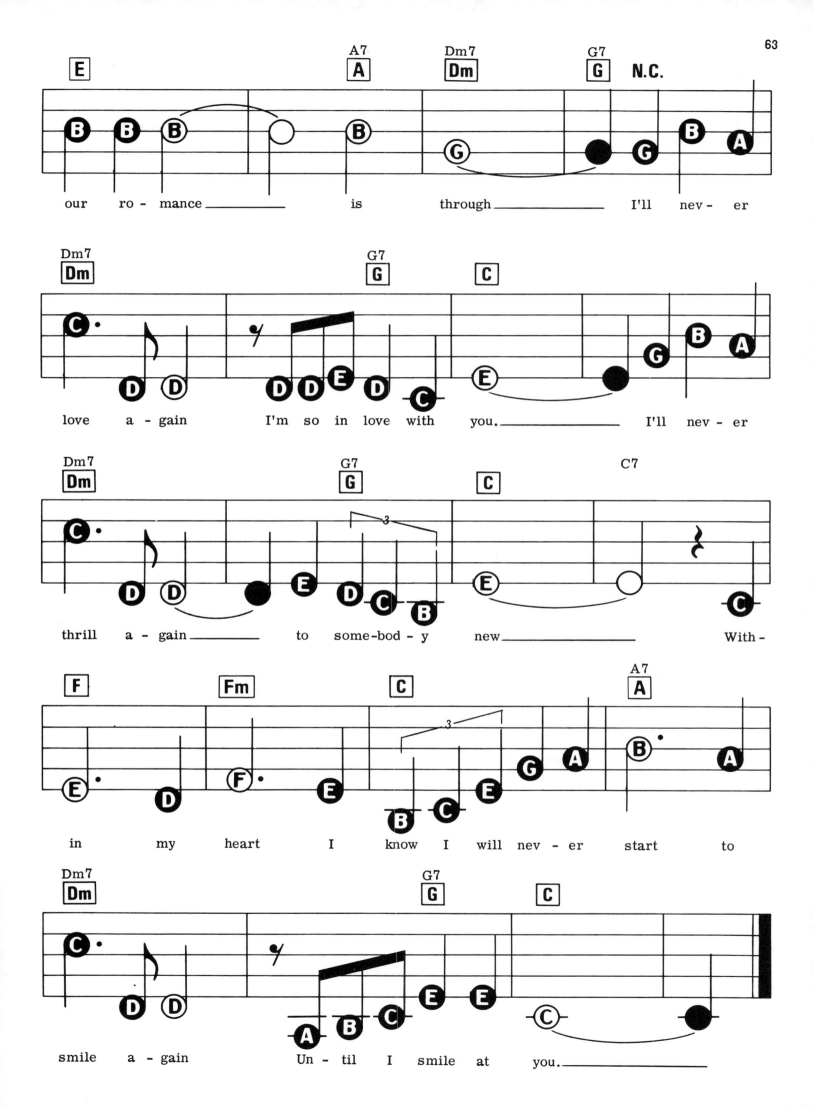

I'll Walk Alone
from the Motion Picture FOLLOW THE BOYS

Registration 3
Rhythm: Fox Trot or Swing

Lyric by Sammy Cahn
Music by Jule Styne

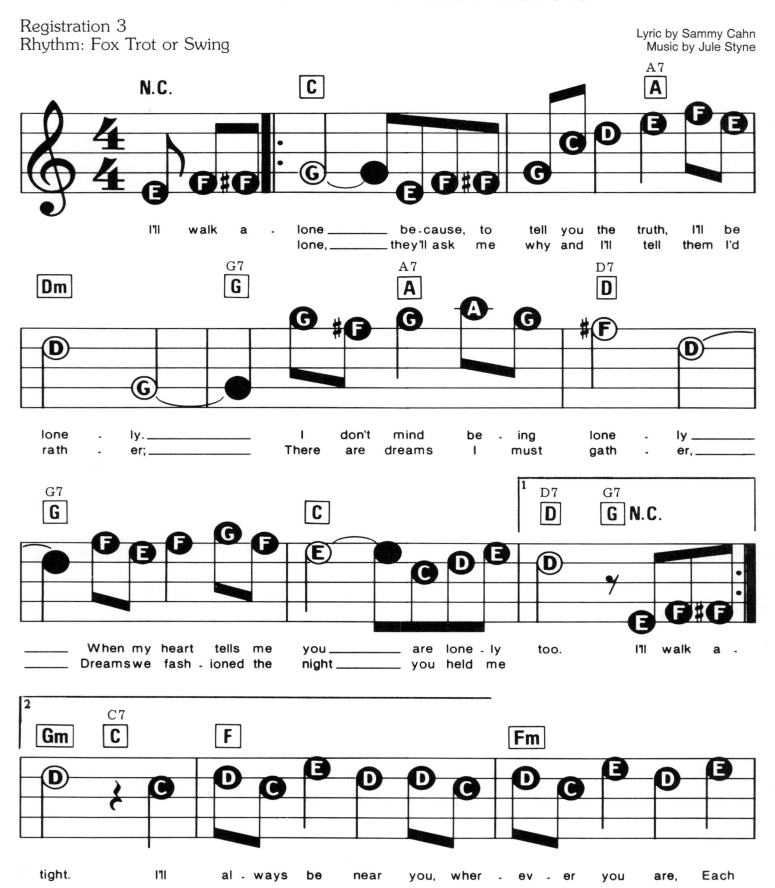

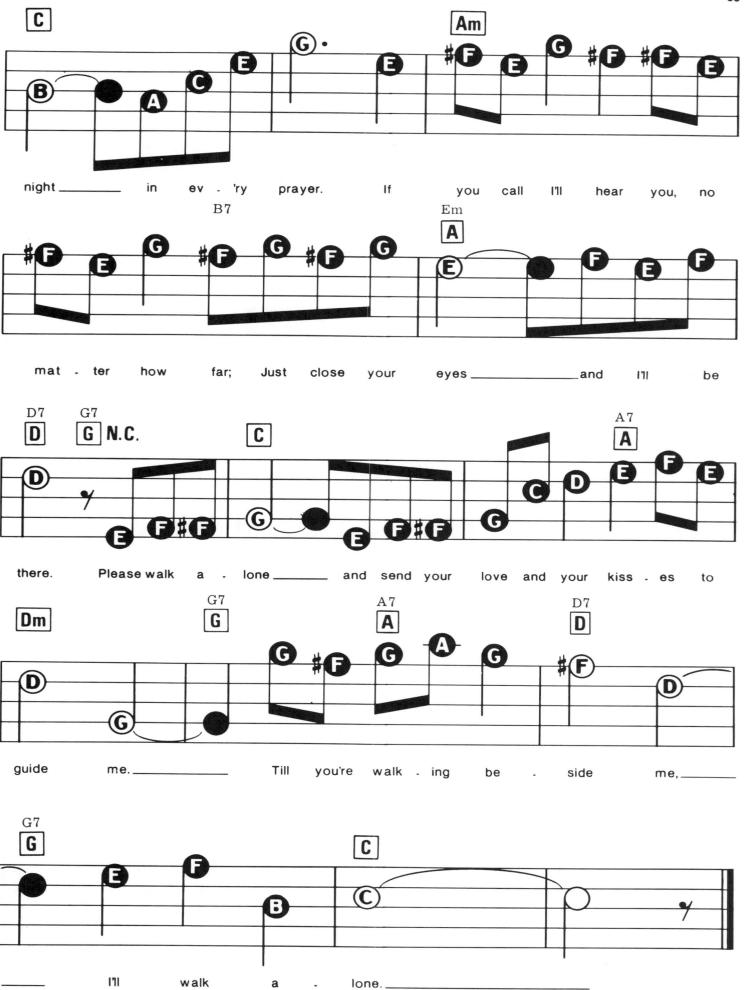

night _____ in ev - 'ry prayer. If you call I'll hear you, no

mat - ter how far; Just close your eyes _____ and I'll be

there. Please walk a - lone _____ and send your love and your kiss - es to

guide me. _____ Till you're walk - ing be - side me, _____

_____ I'll walk a - lone. _____

I'm Beginning To See The Light

Registration 4
Rhythm: Fox Trot or Swing

Words and Music by Don George, Johnny Hodges,
Duke Ellington and Harry James

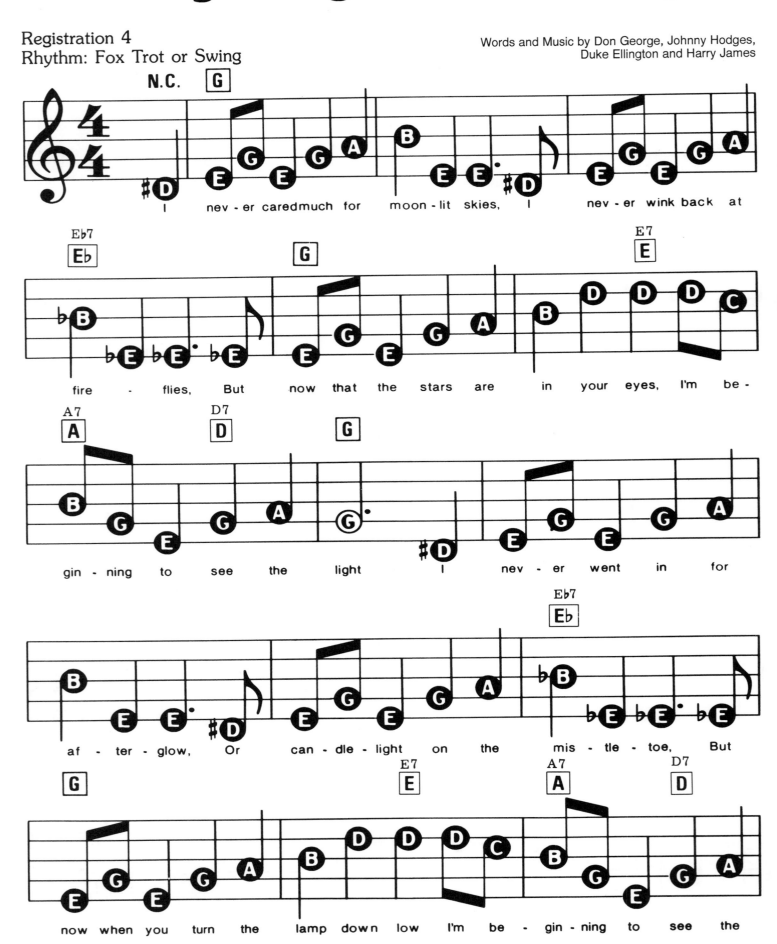

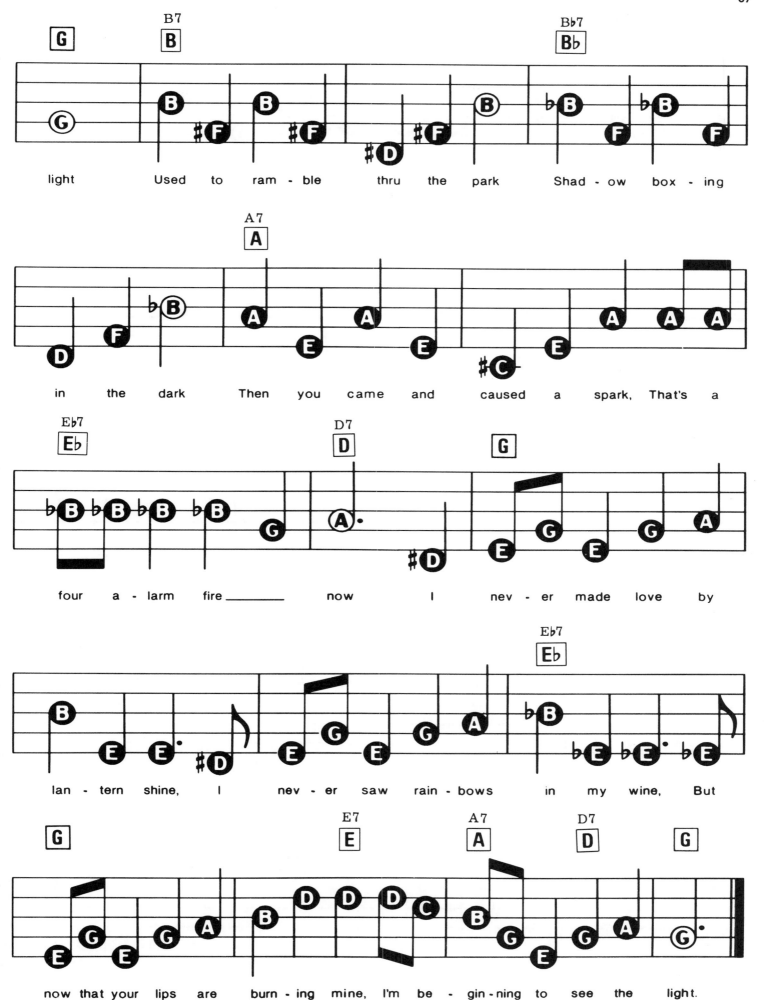

Is You Is, Or Is You Ain't
(Ma' Baby)
from FOLLOW THE BOYS

Registration 1
Rhythm: Jazz or Swing

Words and Music by Billy Austin
and Louis Jordan

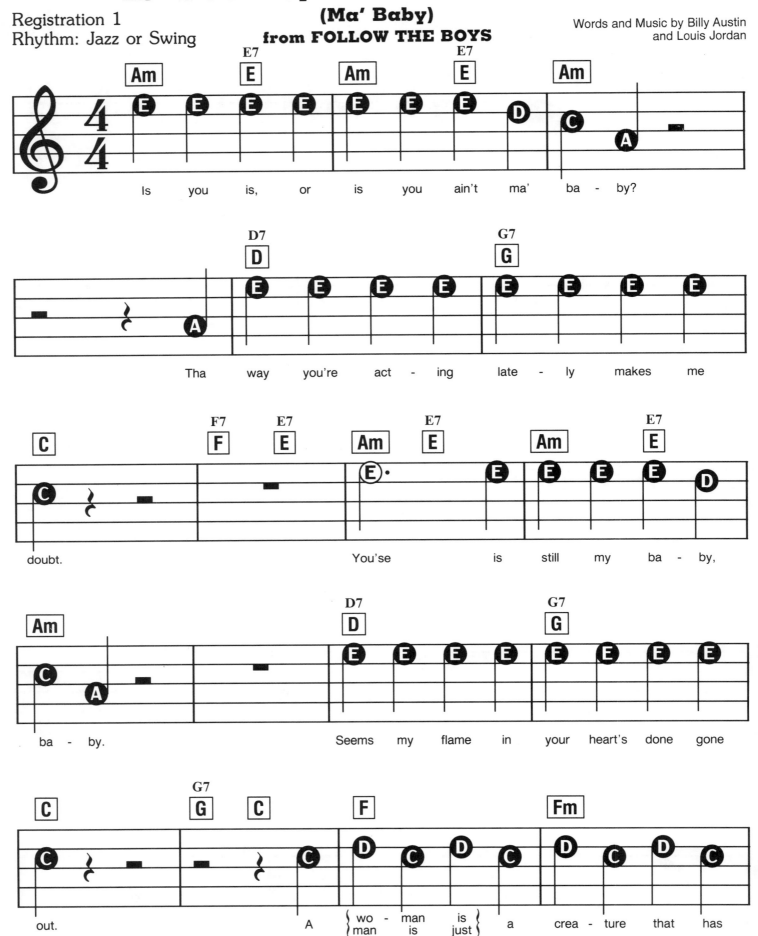

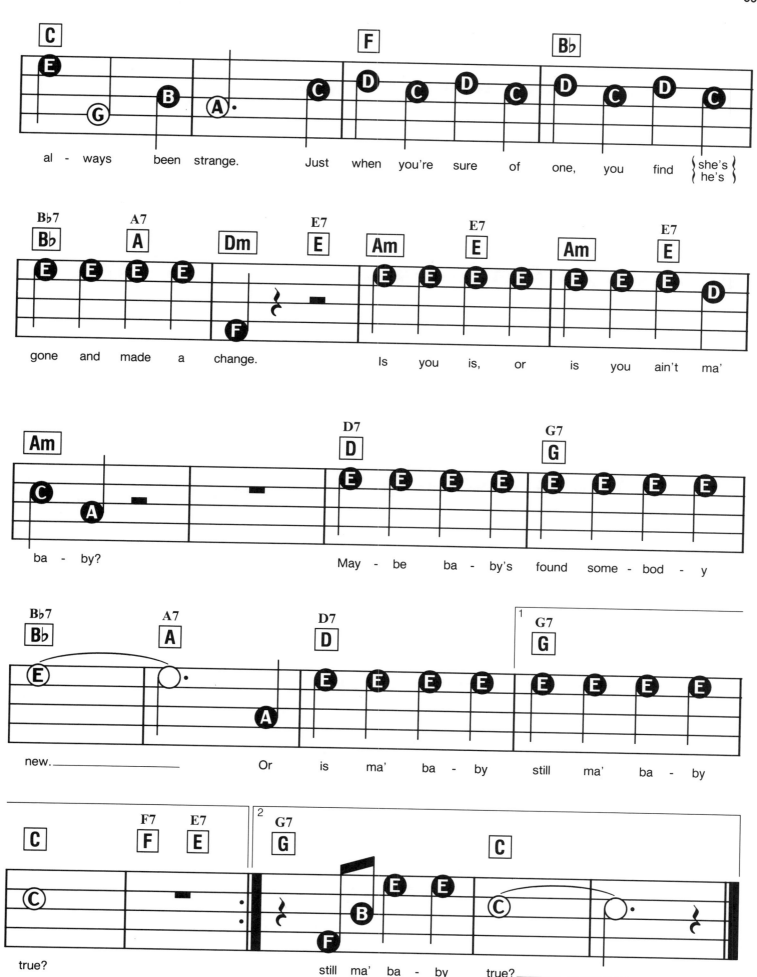

C F B♭
al - ways been strange. Just when you're sure of one, you find { she's / he's }
B♭7 B♭ A7 A Dm E7 E Am E7 E Am E7 E
gone and made a change. Is you is, or is you ain't ma'
Am D7 D G7 G
ba - by? May - be ba - by's found some - bod - y
B♭7 B♭ A7 A D7 D 1 G7 G
new. Or is ma' ba - by still ma' ba - by
C F7 F E7 E 2 G7 G C
true? still ma' ba - by true?

It's Been A Long, Long Time

Registration 9
Rhythm: Fox Trot or Swing

Lyric by Sammy Cahn
Music by Jule Styne

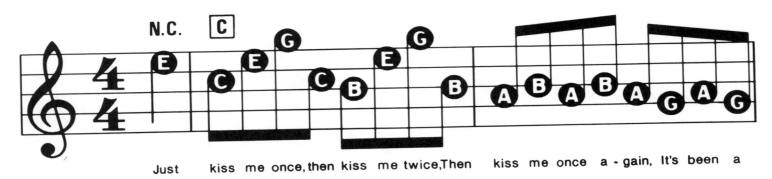

Just kiss me once, then kiss me twice, Then kiss me once a-gain, It's been a

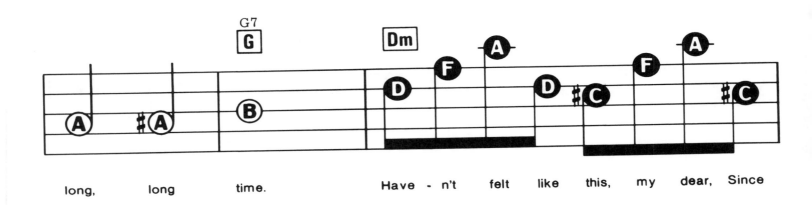

long, long time. Have-n't felt like this, my dear, Since

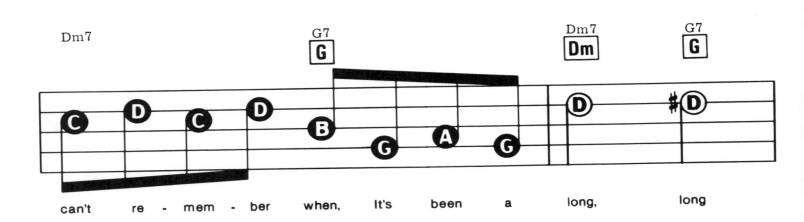

can't re-mem-ber when, It's been a long, long

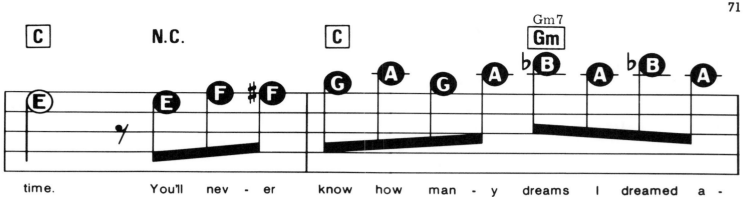

time.　You'll nev - er　know how man - y dreams I dreamed a -

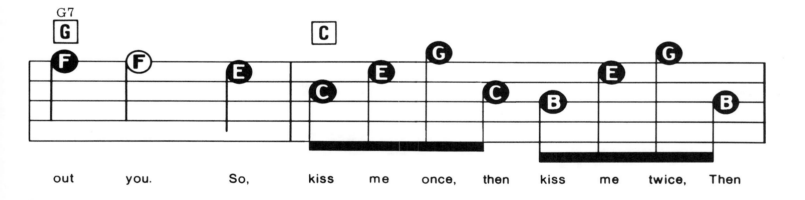

bout you　Or　just how emp - ty they all seemed with -

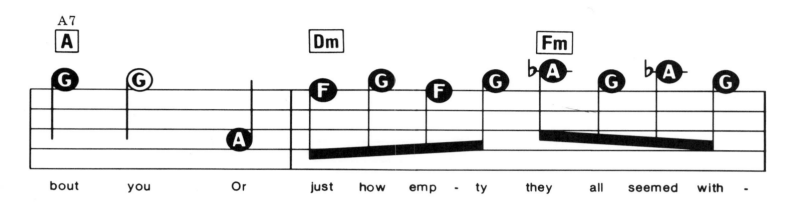

out you.　So, kiss me once, then kiss me twice, Then

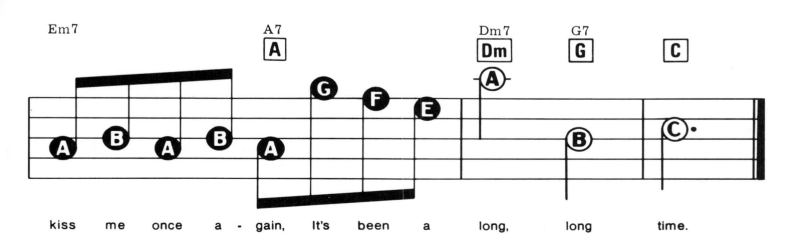

kiss me once a - gain, It's been a long, long time.

In The Blue Of Evening

Registration 3
Rhythm: Fox Trot or Swing

Words by Tom Adair
Music by D'Artega

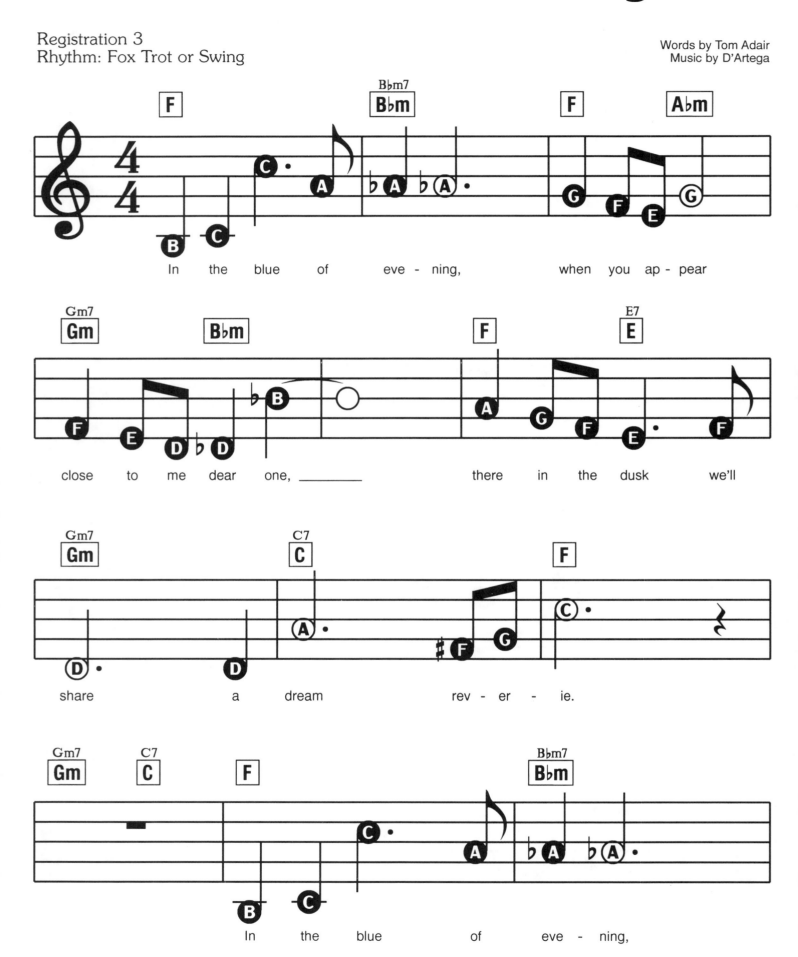

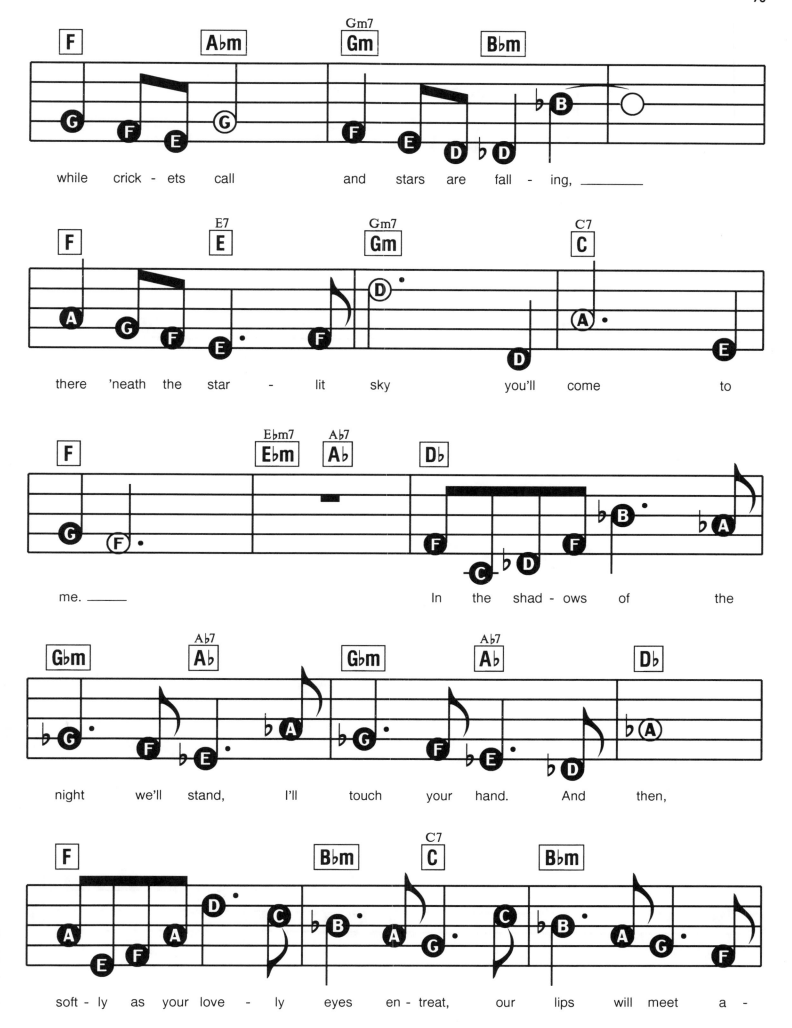

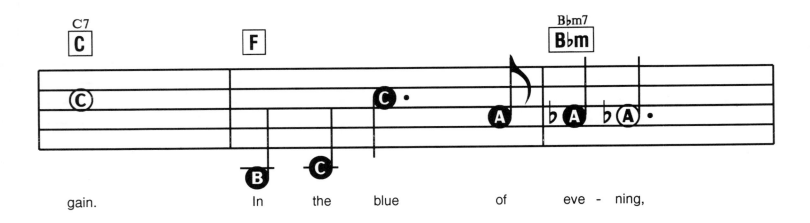

gain.   In the blue of eve - ning,

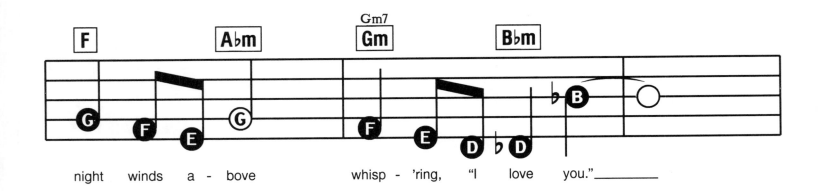

night winds a - bove   whisp - 'ring, "I love you."_____

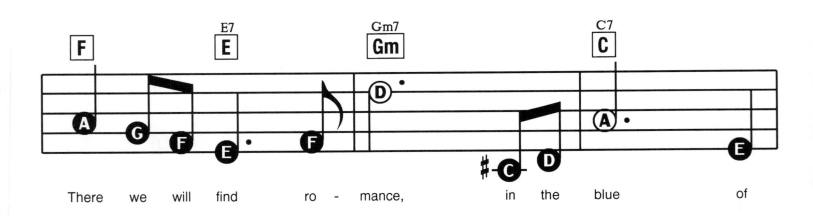

There we will find ro - mance,   in the blue of

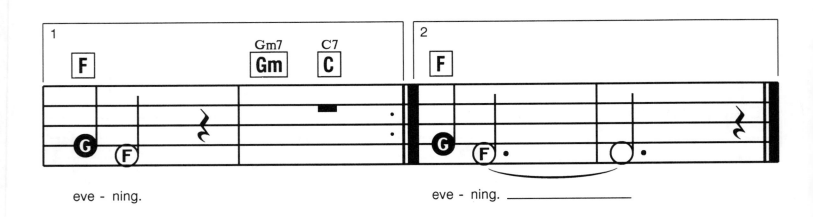

eve - ning.   eve - ning. _____

Kiss The Boys Goodbye

Theme from the Paramount Picture
KISS THE BOYS GOODBYE

Registration 4
Rhythm: Fox Trot or Swing

Words by Frank Loesser
Music by Victor Schertzinger

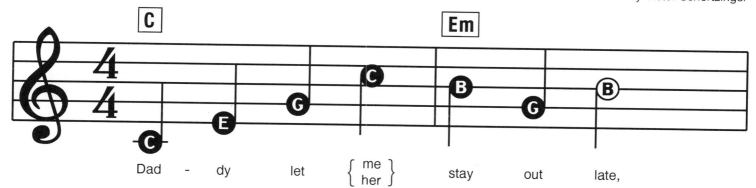

Dad - dy let { me her } stay out late,

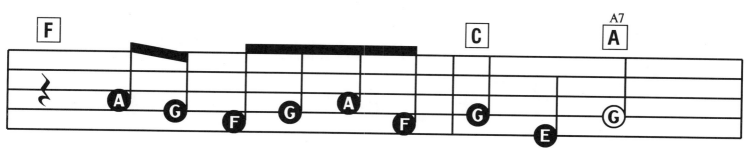

for to - mor - row is { our her } wed - ding date.

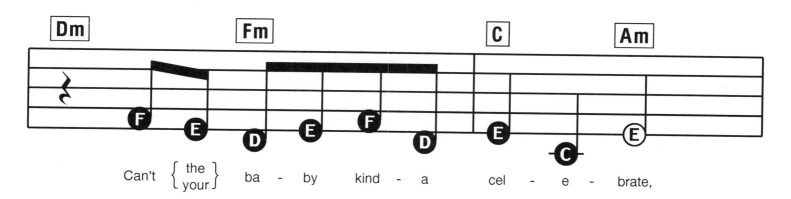

Can't { the your } ba - by kind - a cel - e - brate,

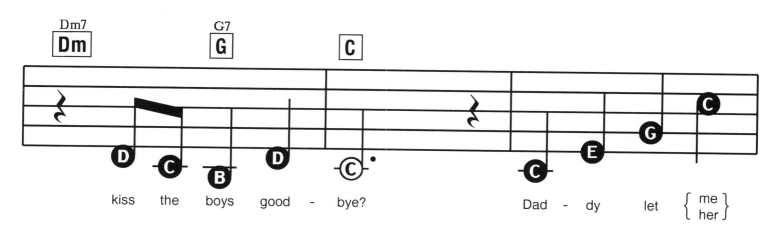

kiss the boys good - bye?   Dad - dy let { me her }

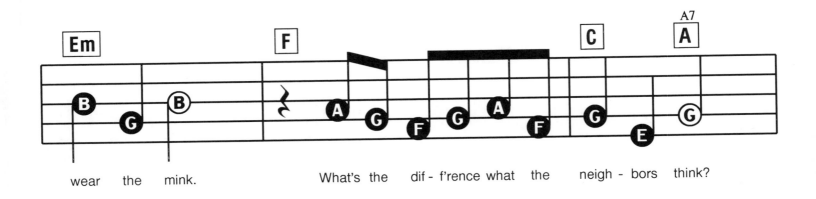

wear   the   mink.   What's the dif - f'rence what   the   neigh - bors think?

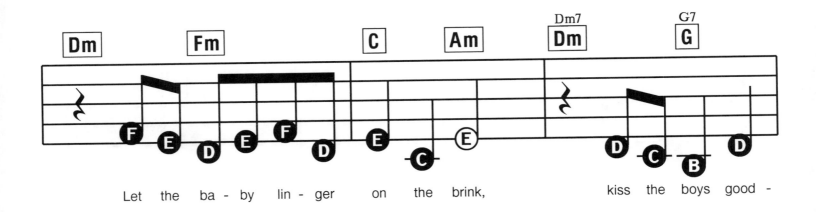

Let   the   ba - by   lin - ger   on   the   brink,   kiss   the   boys good -

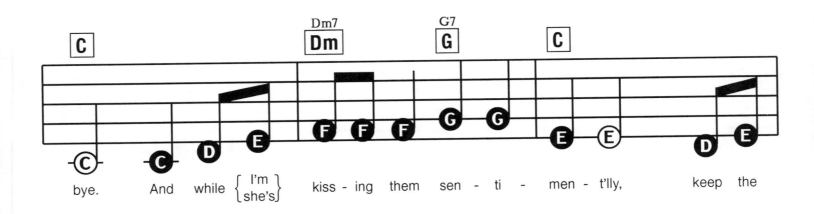

bye.   And   while {I'm / she's}   kiss - ing them sen - ti - men - t'lly,   keep the

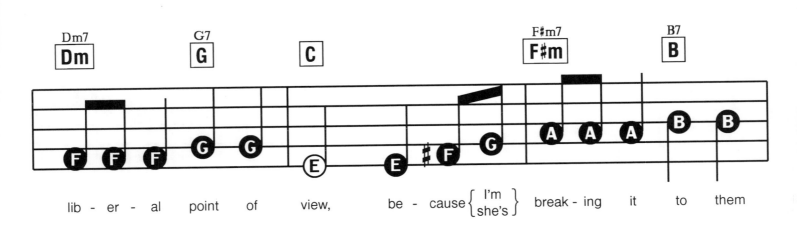

lib - er - al   point   of   view,   be - cause {I'm / she's} break - ing it   to   them

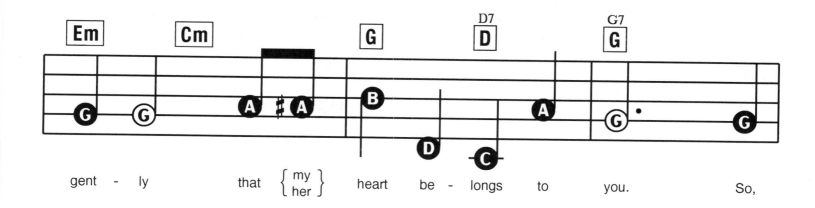

gent - ly that { my / her } heart be - longs to you. So,

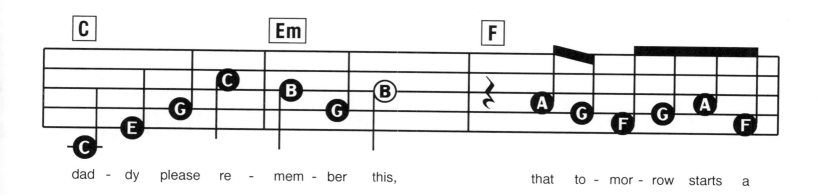

dad - dy please re - mem - ber this, that to - mor - row starts a

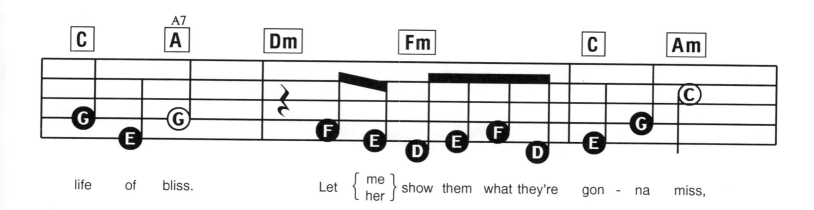

life of bliss. Let { me / her } show them what they're gon - na miss,

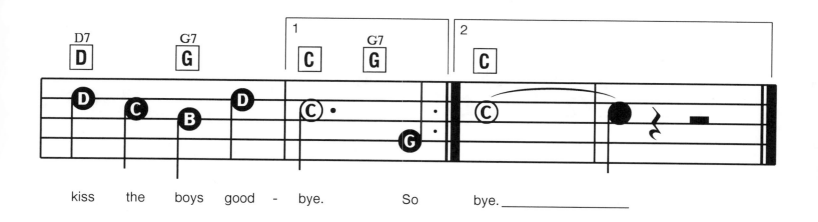

kiss the boys good - bye. So bye. _____

Juke Box Saturday Night

from STARS ON ICE

Words by Al Stillman
Music by Paul McGrane

Registration 4
Rhythm: Swing

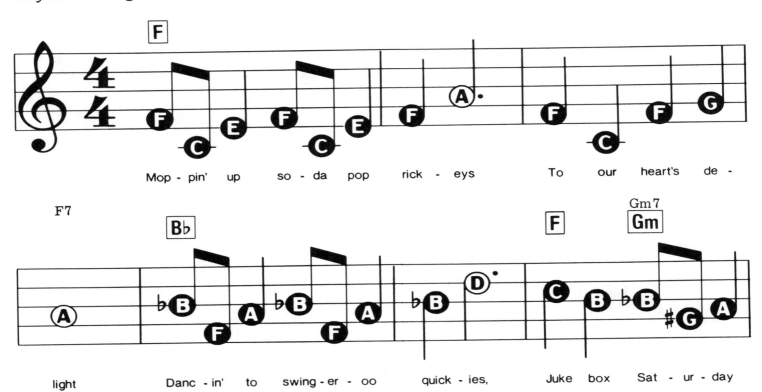

Mop - pin' up so - da pop rick - eys   To our heart's de -

light   Danc - in' to swing - er - oo quick - ies,   Juke box Sat - ur - day

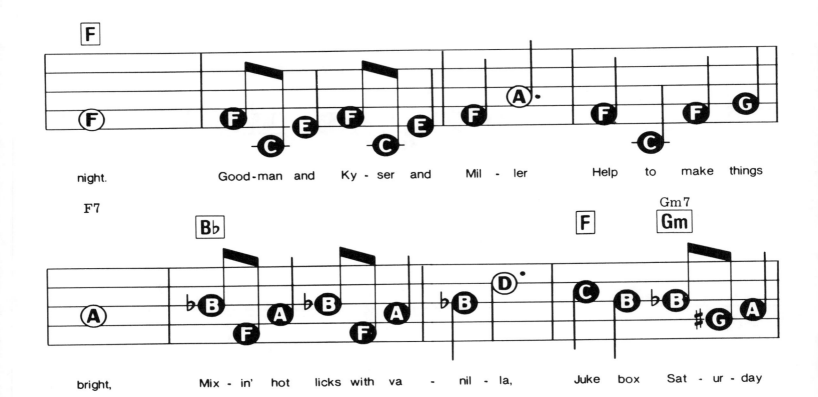

night.   Good - man and Ky - ser and Mil - ler   Help to make things

bright,   Mix - in' hot licks with va - nil - la,   Juke box Sat - ur - day

The Last Time I Saw Paris

from LADY, BE GOOD

Registration 10
Rhythm: Ballad or Swing

Lyrics by Oscar Hammerstein II
Music by Jerome Kern

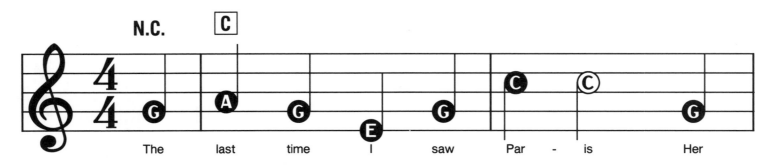

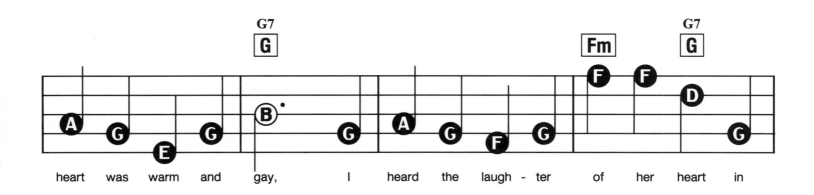

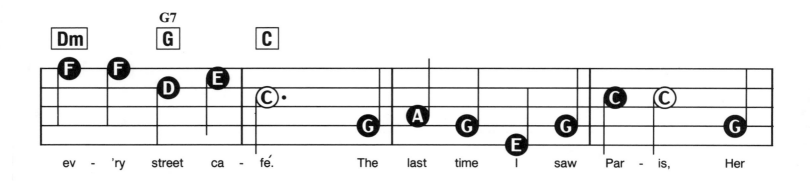

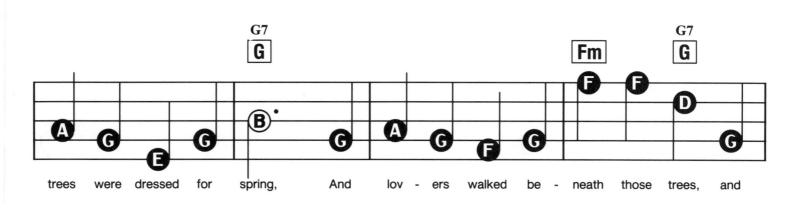

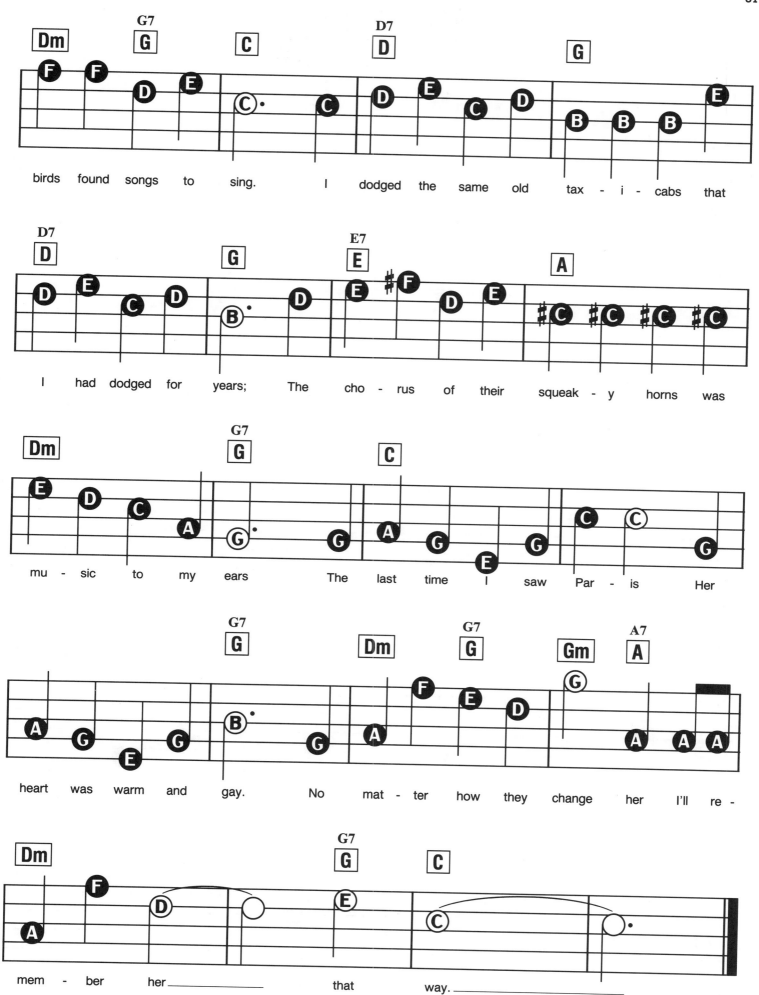

Long Ago
(And Far Away)
from COVER GIRL

Words by Ira Gershwin
Music by Jerome Kern

Registration 3
Rhythm: Ballad or Swing

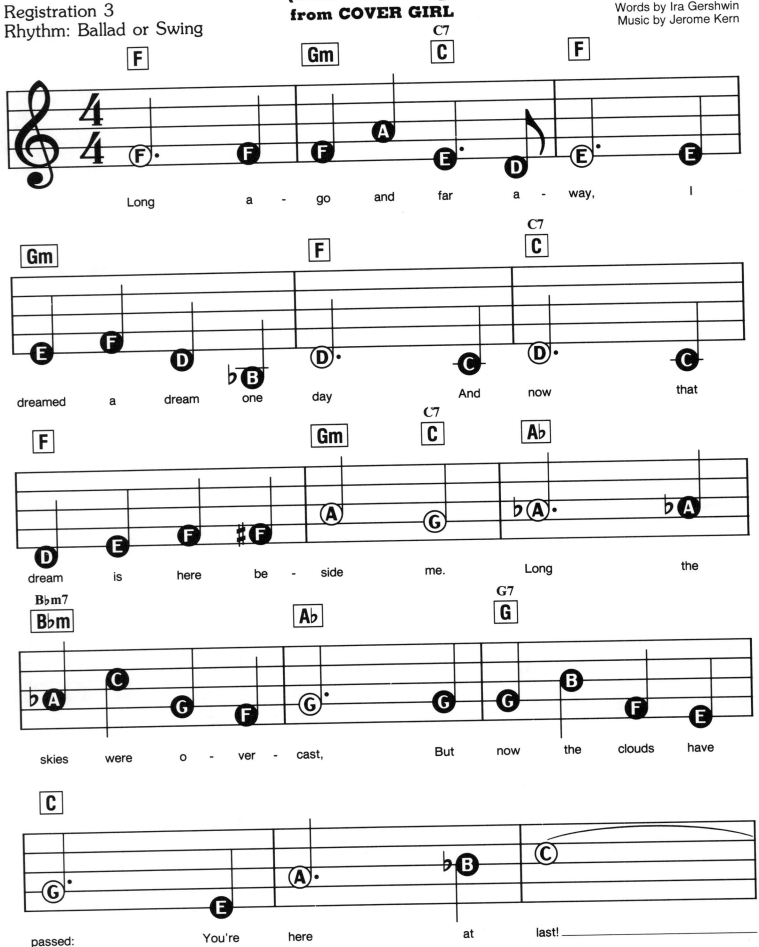

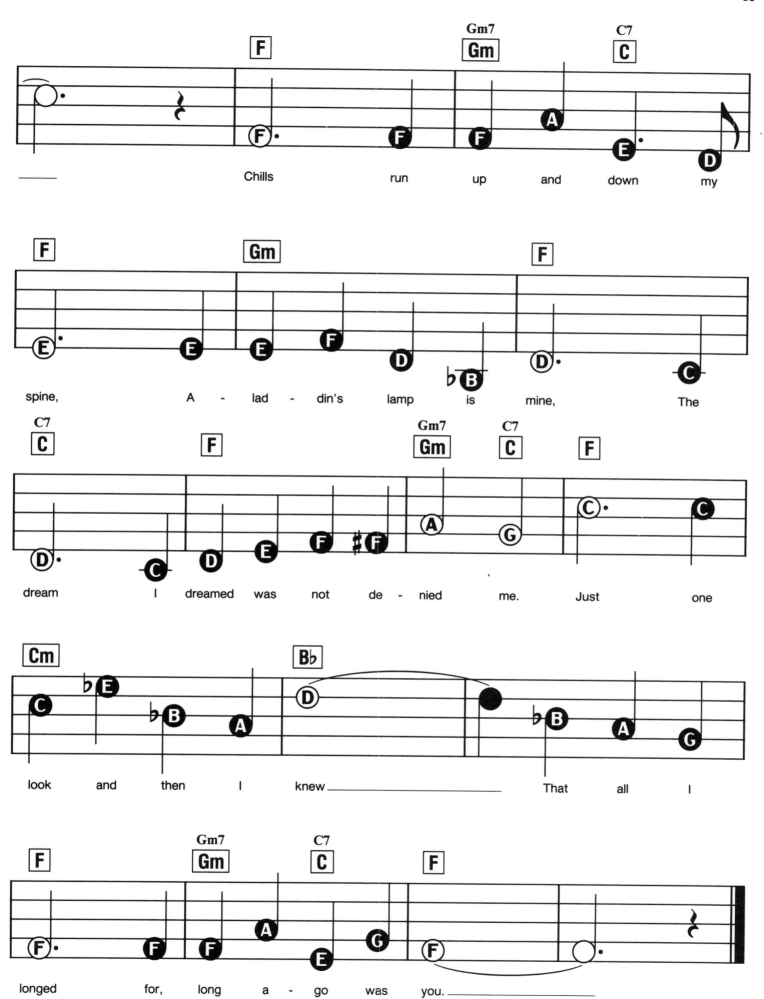

Love Letters
Theme from the Paramount Picture LOVE LETTERS

Registration 1
Rhythm: Swing

Words by Edward Heyman
Music by Victor Young

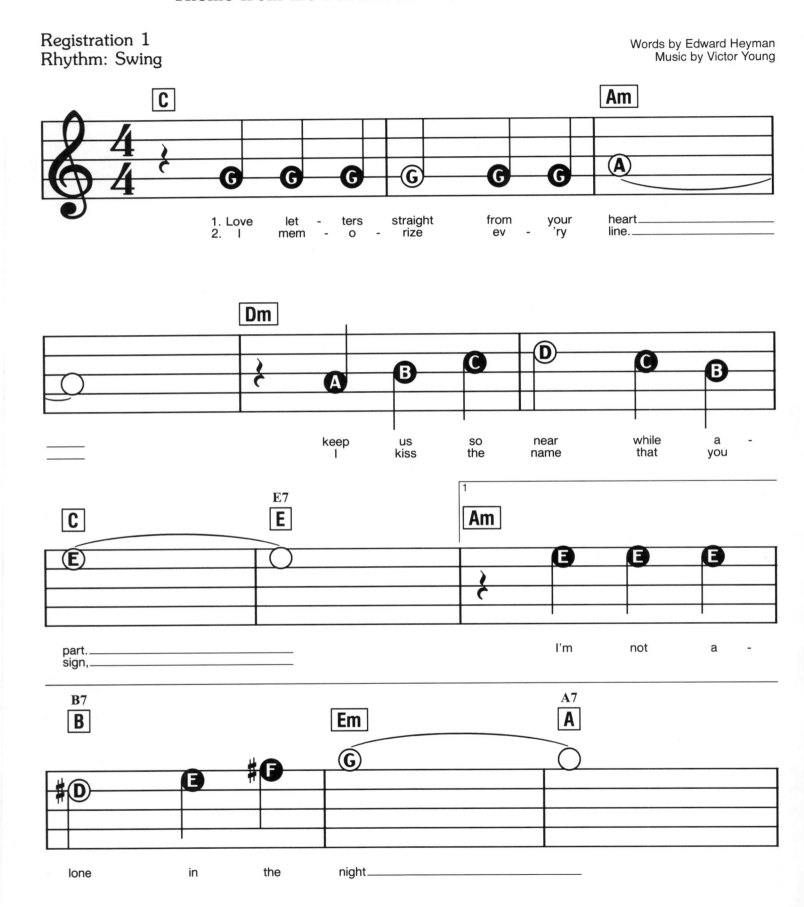

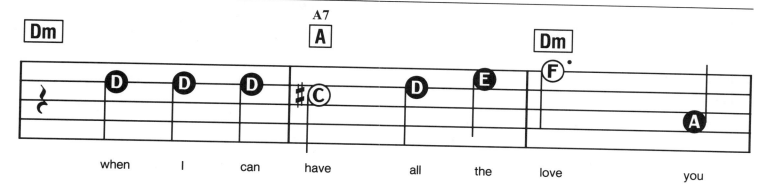

when I can have all the love you

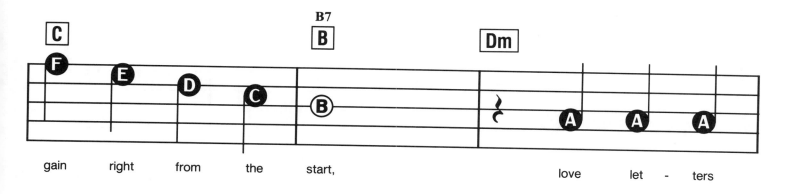

write. and dar - ling, then I read a -

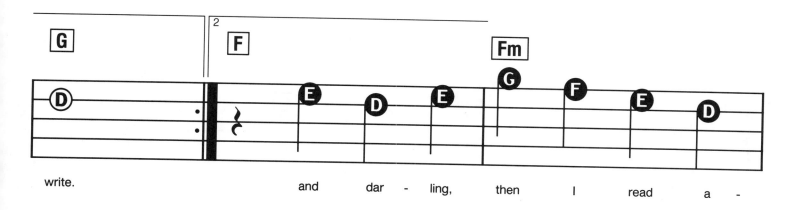

gain right from the start, love let - ters

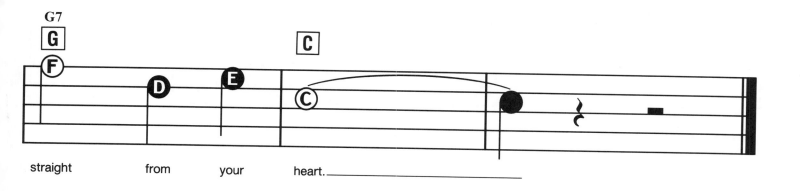

straight from your heart.

Moonlight Becomes You
from the Paramount Picture ROAD TO MOROCCO

Registration 1
Rhythm: Swing

Words by Johnny Burke
Music by James Van Heusen

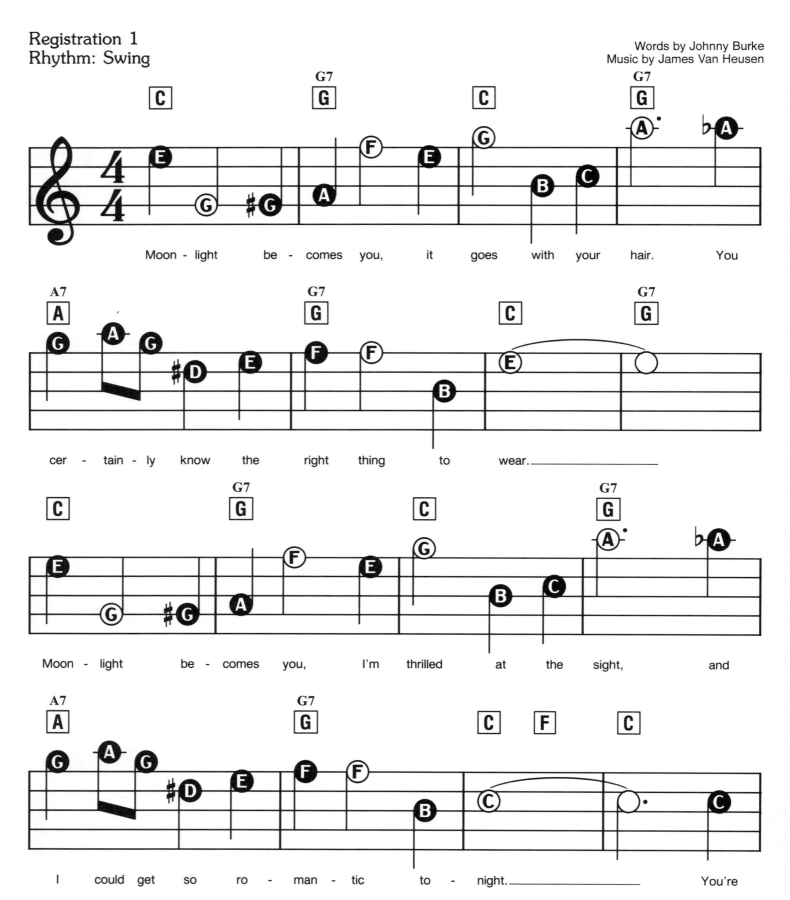

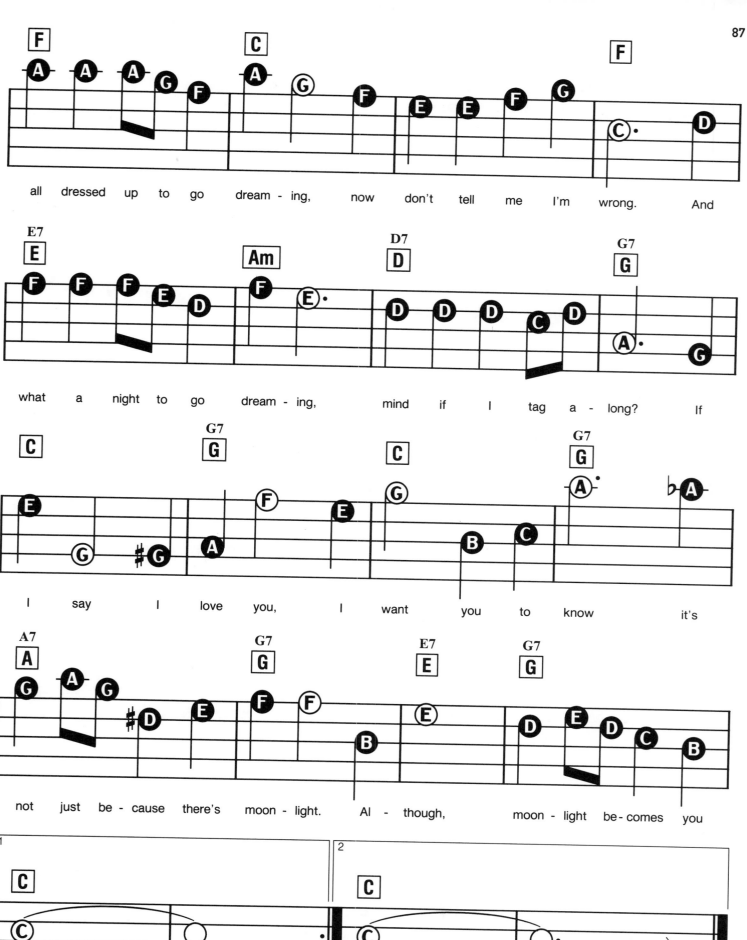

all dressed up to go dream - ing, now don't tell me I'm wrong. And

what a night to go dream - ing, mind if I tag a - long? If

I say I love you, I want you to know it's

not just be - cause there's moon - light. Al - though, moon - light be - comes you

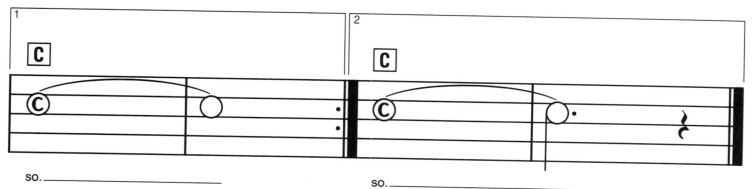

so._____ so._____

Moonlight In Vermont

Registration 2
Rhythm: Fox Trot or Swing

Words and Music by John Blackburn
and Karl Suessdorf

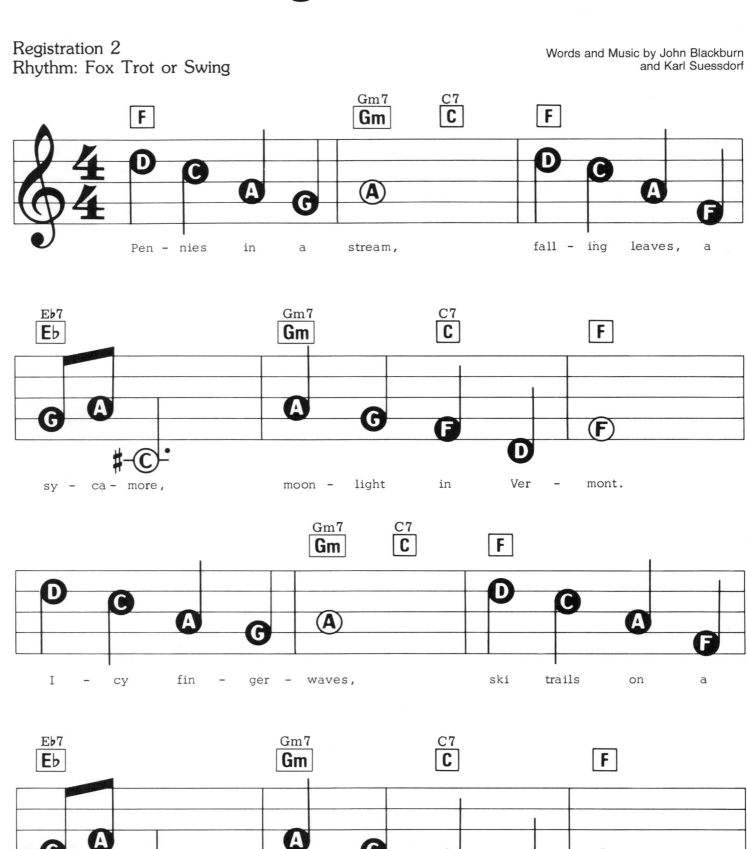

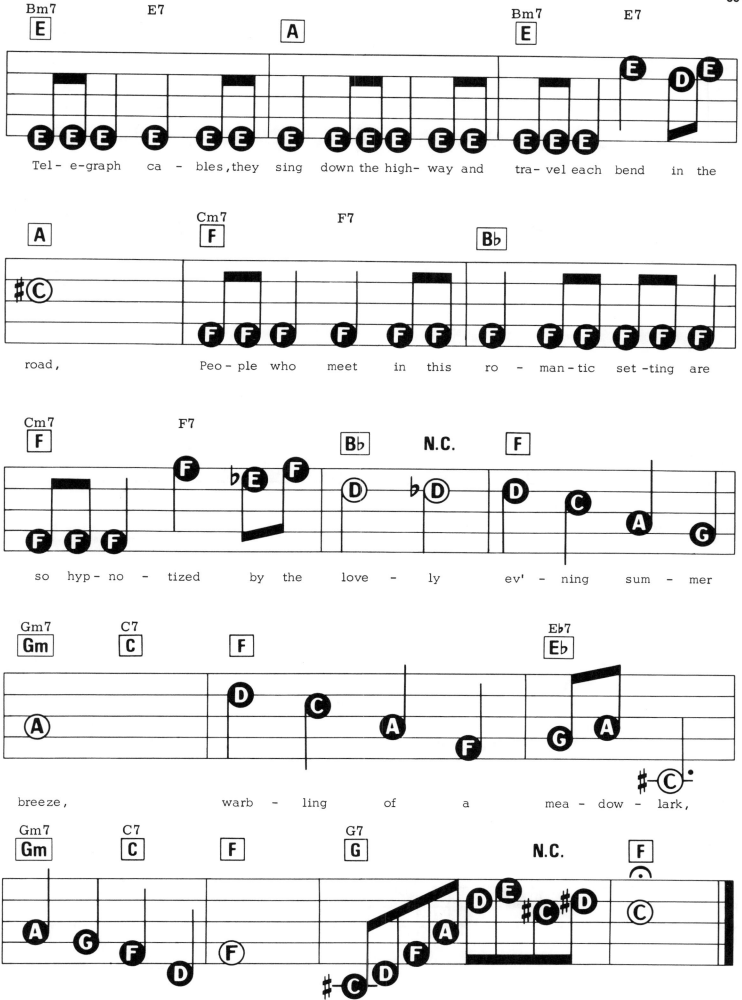

My Shining Hour

from the Motion Picture THE SKY'S THE LIMIT

Registration 7
Rhythm: Fox Trot or Swing

Lyric by Johnny Mercer
Music by Harold Arlen

This will be my shin - ing hour _____

calm and hap - py and bright. _____

In my dreams your face will flow - er

through the dark - ness of the night. _____

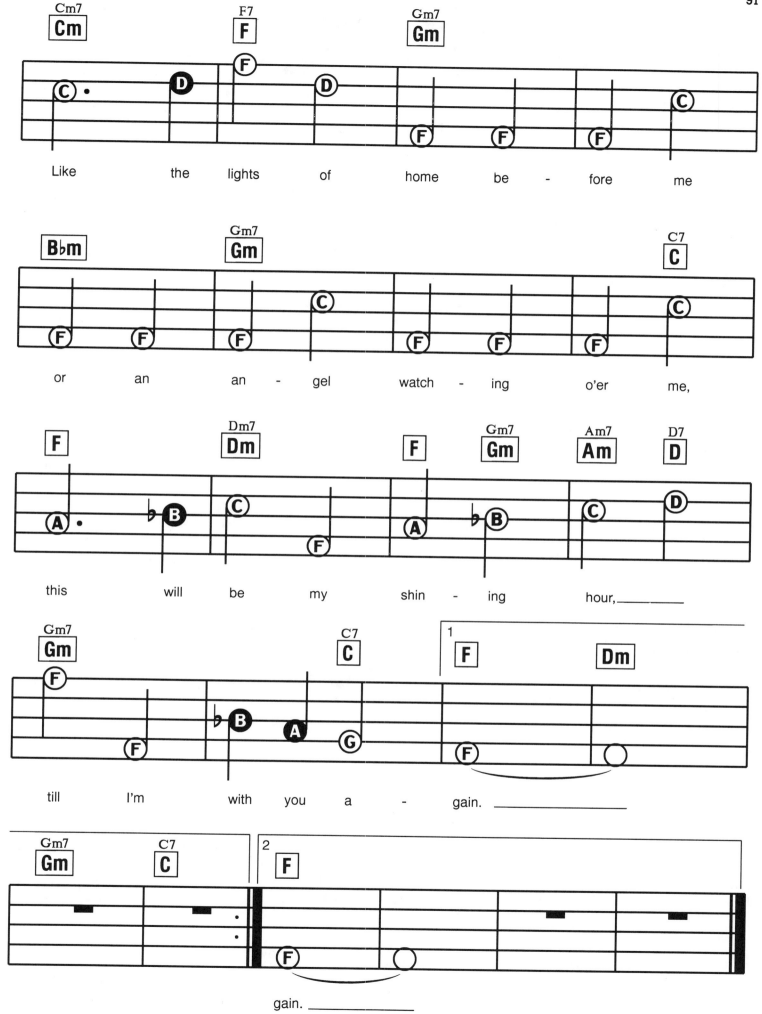

A Nightingale Sang
In Berkeley Square

Registration 2
Rhythm: Ballad

Lyric by Eric Maschwitz
Music by Manning Sherwin

93

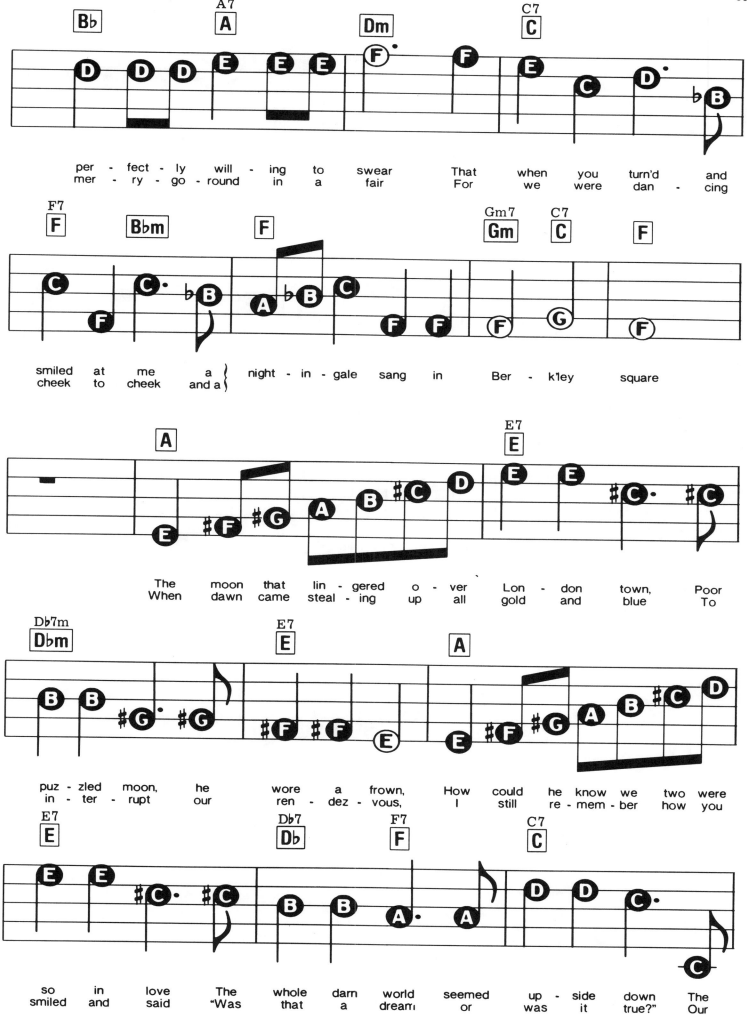

94

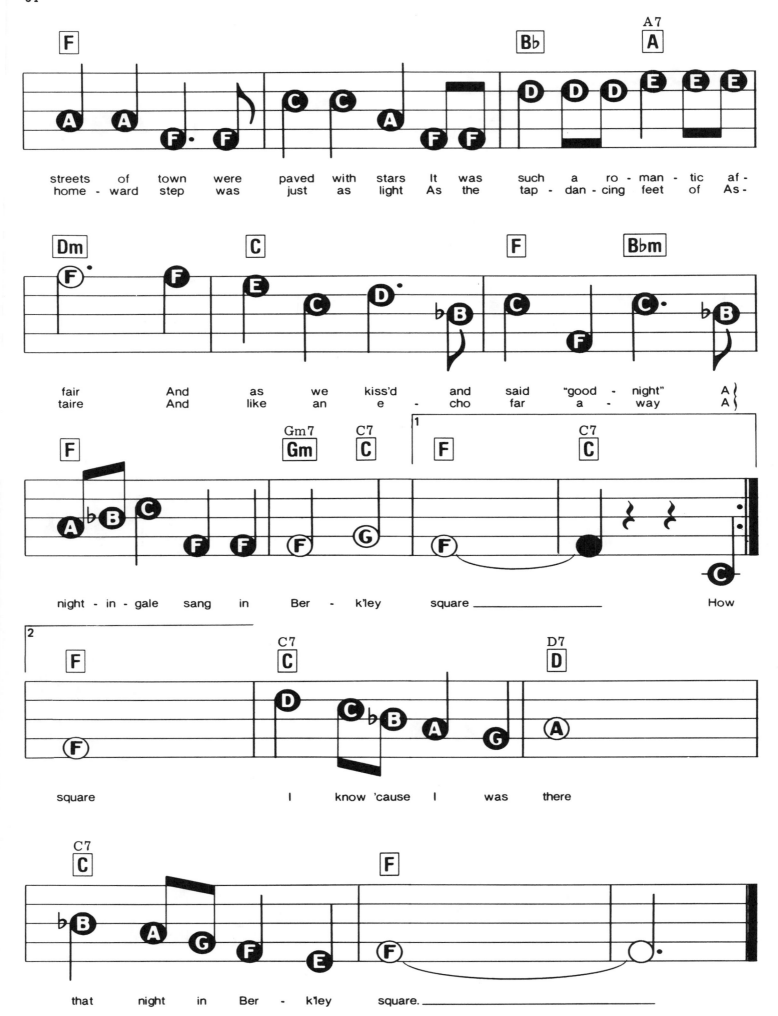

Praise The Lord And Pass The Ammunition!

Registration 4
Rhythm: Fox Trot or Swing

Words and Music by
Frank Loesser

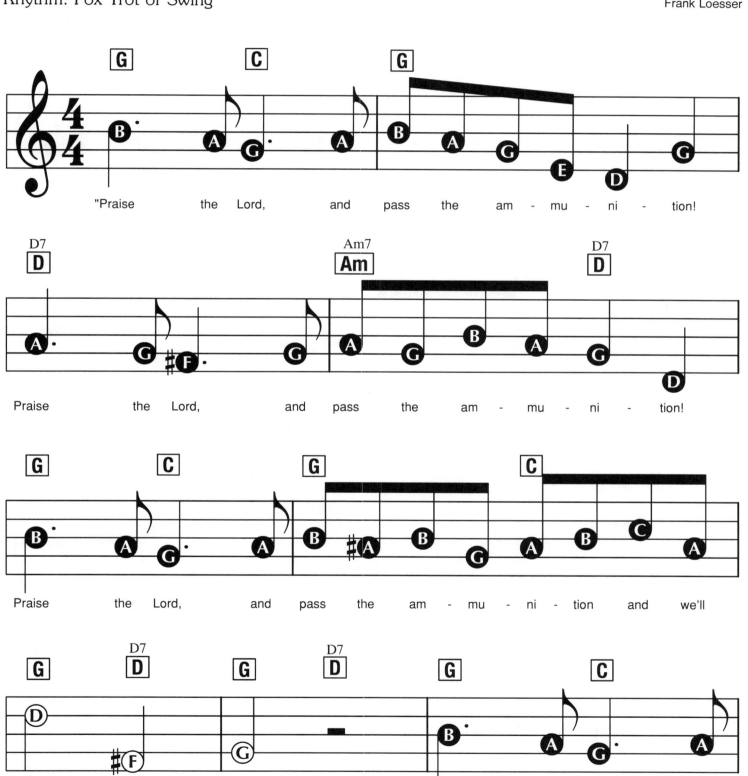

swing in - to po - si - tion, can't af - ford to

sit a - round a - wish - in'. Praise the Lord, we're

all be - tween per - di - tion and the deep blue sea!" Yes the

sky - pi - lot said it you've got to give him cred - it for a

son of a gun of a gun - nee was he. Shout - ing

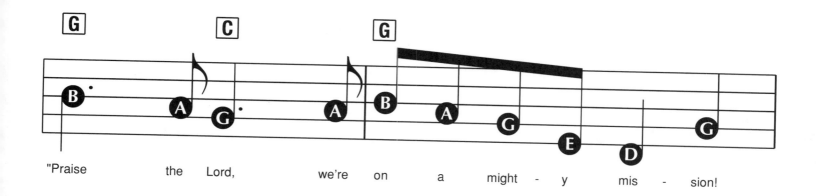

"Praise the Lord, we're on a might - y mis - sion!

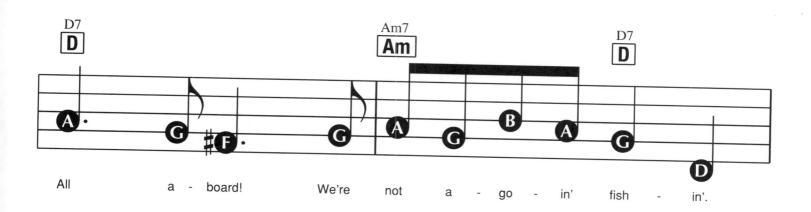

All a - board! We're not a - go - in' fish - in'.

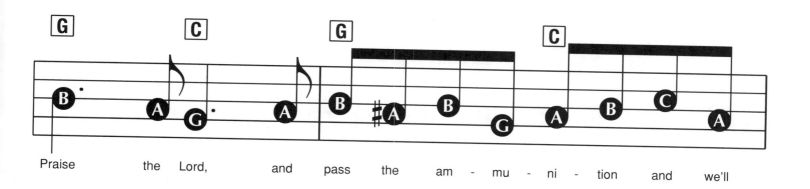

Praise the Lord, and pass the am - mu - ni - tion and we'll

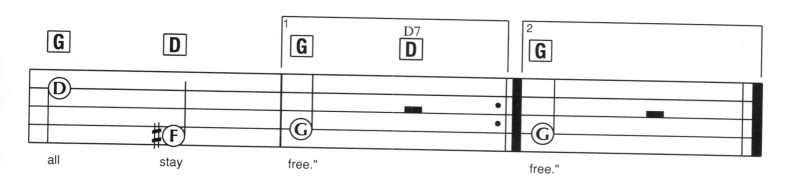

all stay free." free."

One For My Baby
(And One More For The Road)
from the Motion Picture THE SKY'S THE LIMIT

Lyric by Johnny Mercer
Music by Harold Arlen

Registration 2
Rhythm: Fox Trot or Swing

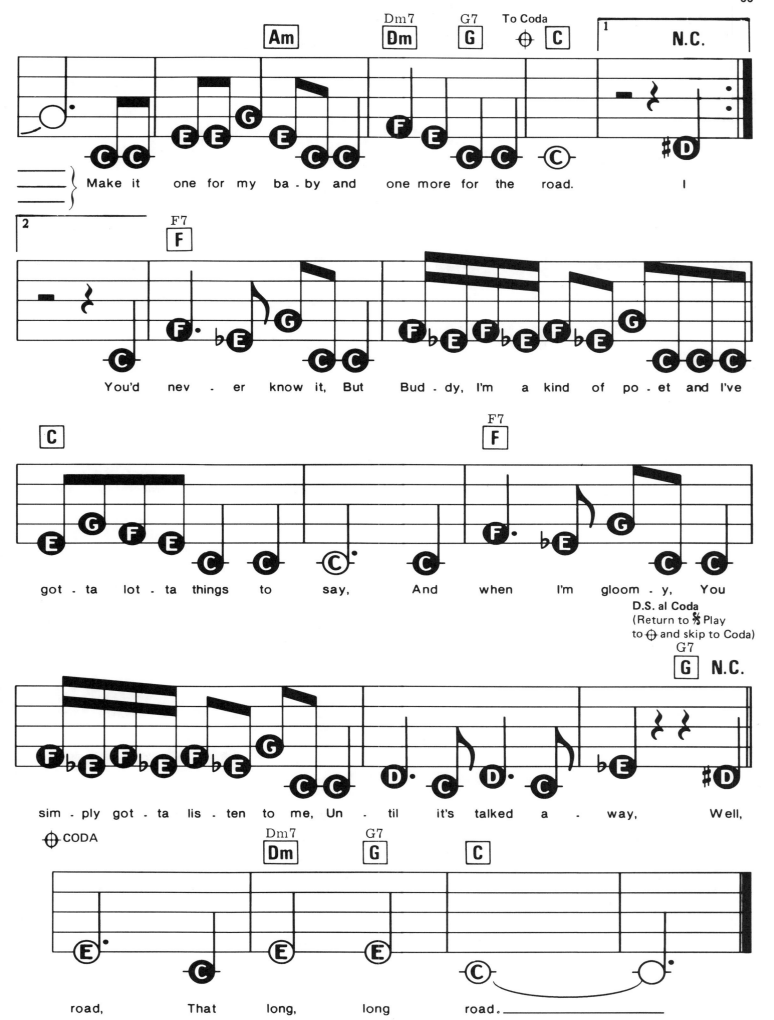

Saturday Night Is The Loneliest Night Of The Week

Registration 7
Rhythm: Swing

Words by Sammy Cahn
Music by Jule Styne

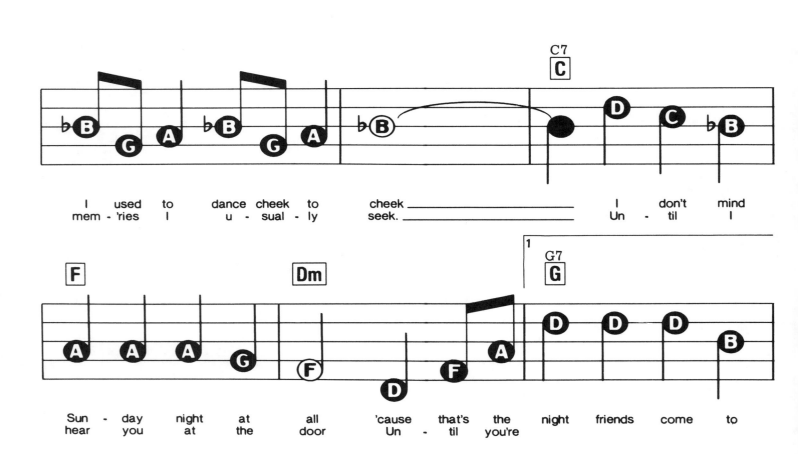

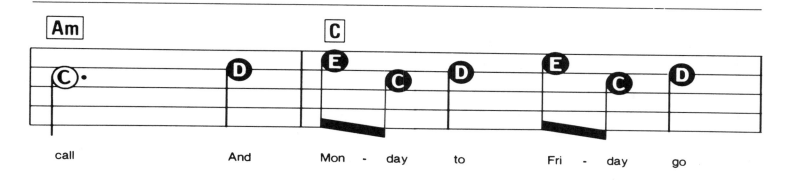

call　　　　　And　　Mon - day　to　　Fri - day　go

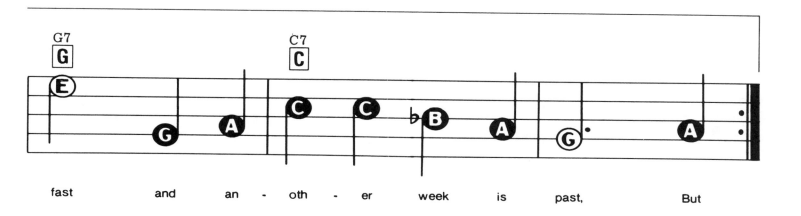

fast　　and　an - oth - er　week　is　past,　　But

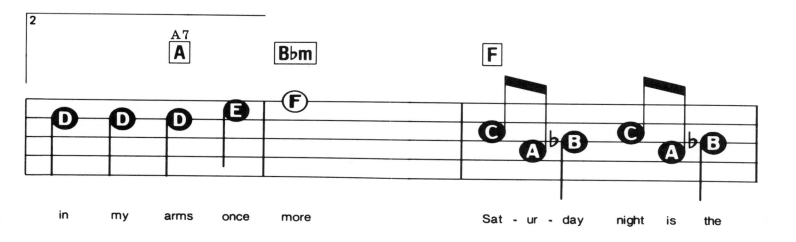

in　my　arms　once　more　　　Sat - ur - day　night　is　the

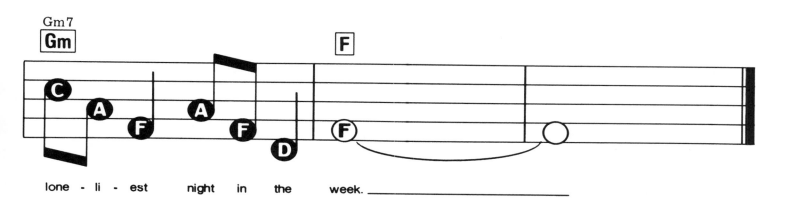

lone - li - est　night　in　the　week.＿＿＿＿

Seems Like Old Times

Registration 5
Rhythm: Swing or Jazz

Lyric and Music by John Jacob Loeb
and Carmen Lombardo

Somebody Else Is Taking My Place

Registration 8
Rhythm: Fox Trot or Swing

Words and Music by Dick Howard,
Bob Ellsworth and Russ Morgan

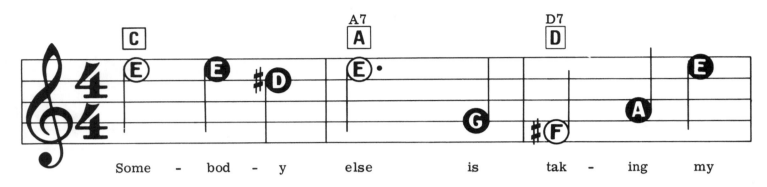

Some - bod - y else is tak - ing my

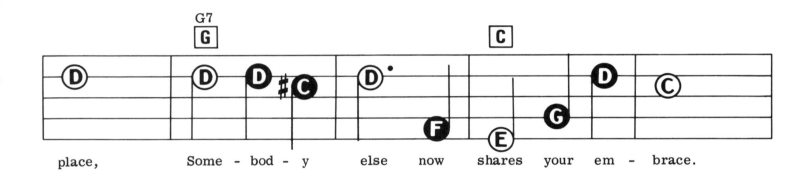

place, Some - bod - y else now shares your em - brace.

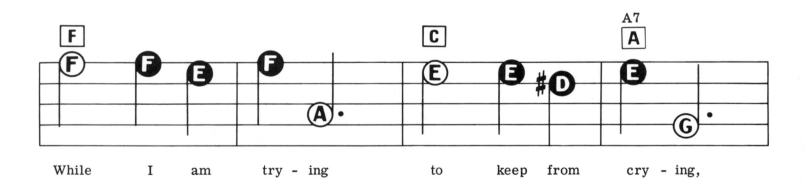

While I am try - ing to keep from cry - ing,

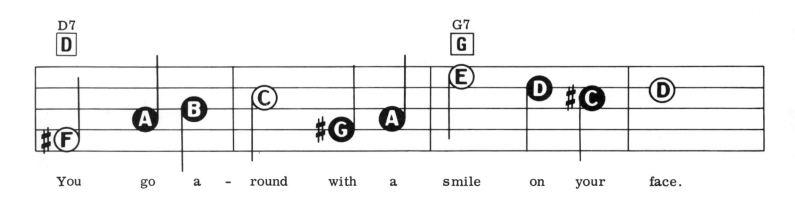

You go a - round with a smile on your face.

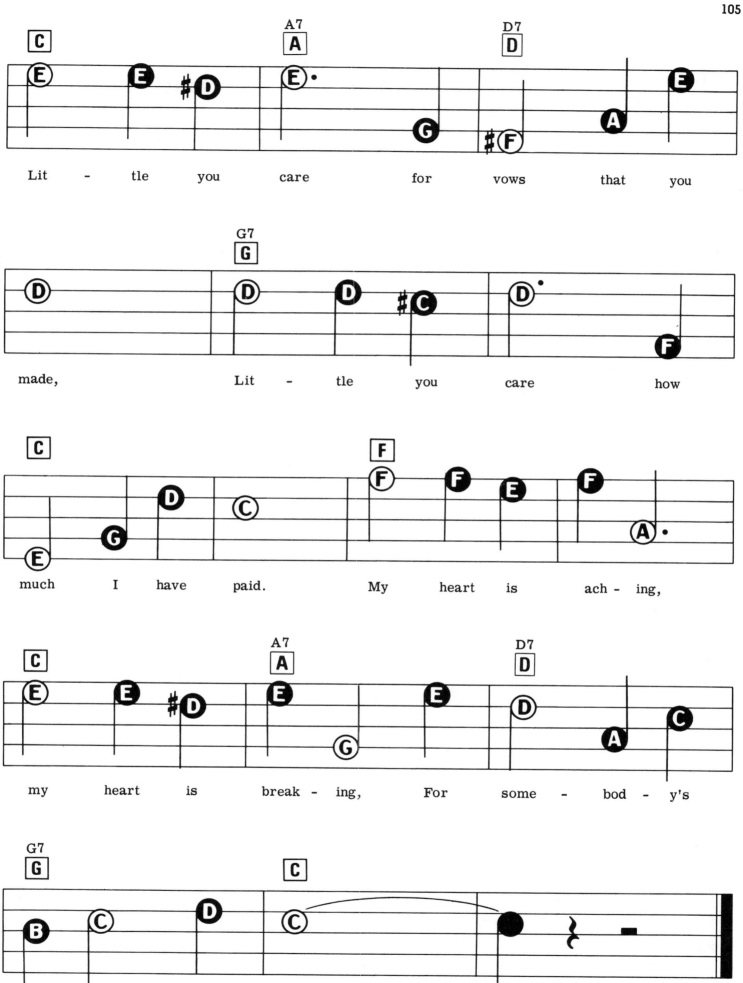

Spring Will Be A Little Late This Year

from the Motion Picture CHRISTMAS HOLIDAY

By Frank Loesser

Registration 4
Rhythm: Fox Trot or Swing

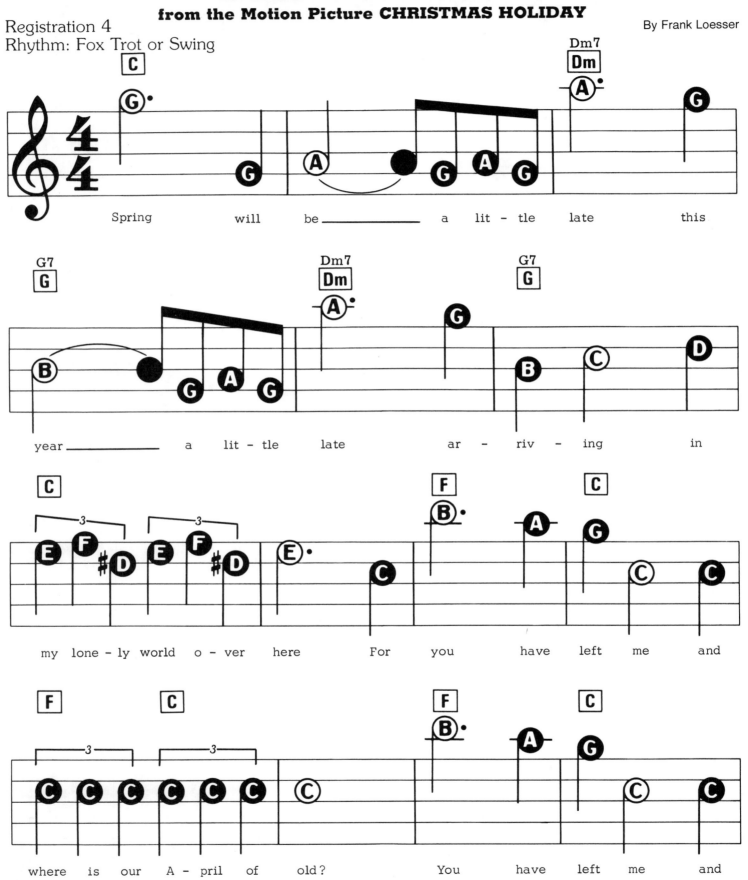

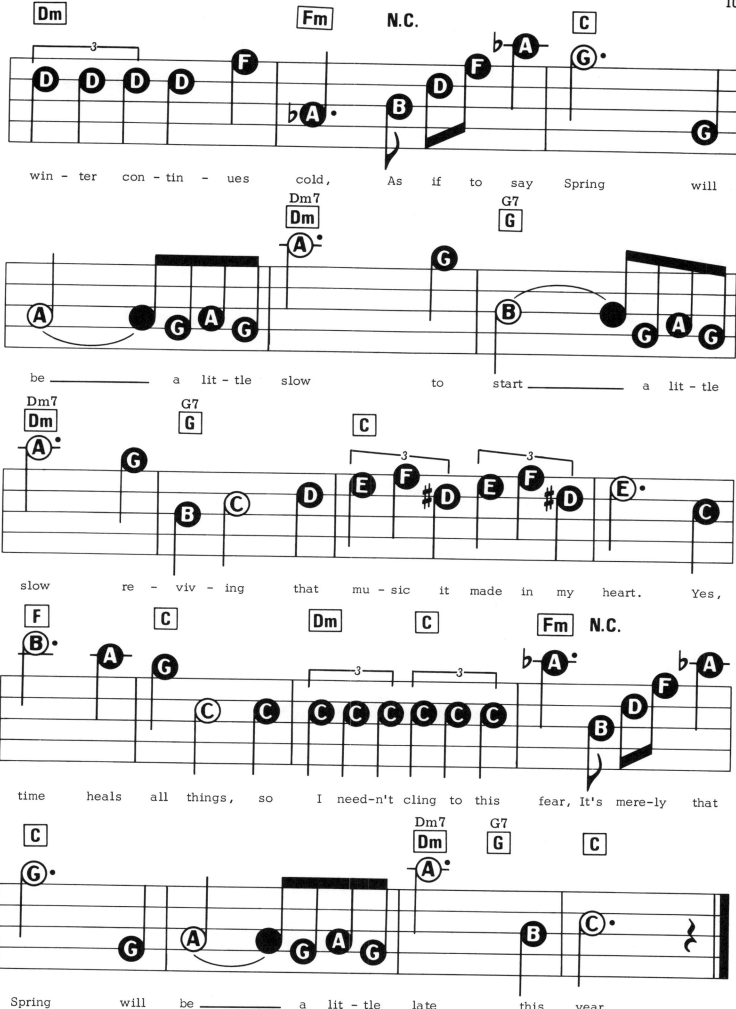

A String Of Pearls

Registration 4
Rhythm: Swing

Words by Eddie DeLange
Music by Jerry Gray

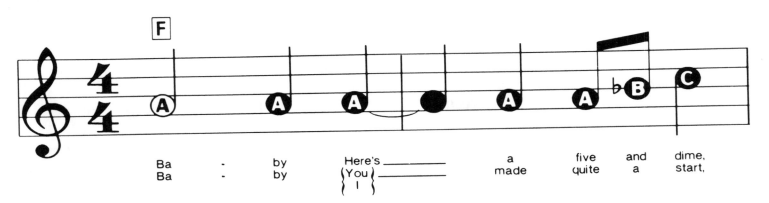

Ba - by Here's _____ a made five and dime,
Ba - by (You) _____ I made quite a start,

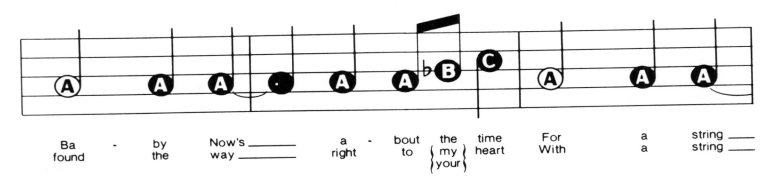

Ba - by Now's _____ a - bout the time For a string _____
found by the way _____ right to (my) heart With a string _____
(your)

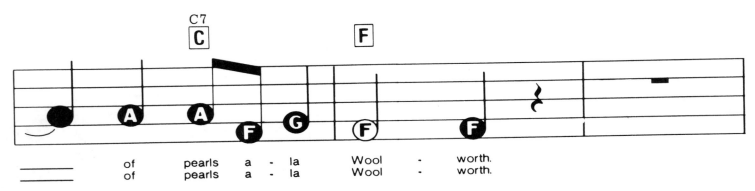

_____ of pearls a la Wool - worth.
_____ of pearls a la Wool - worth.

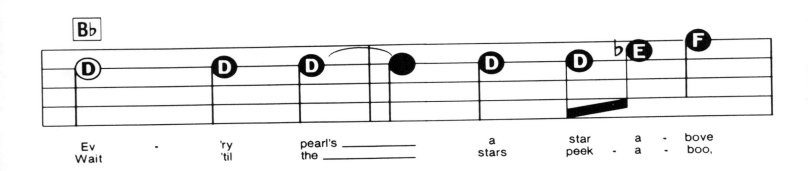

Ev - 'ry pearl's _____ a star a - bove
Wait - 'til the _____ stars peek - a - boo,

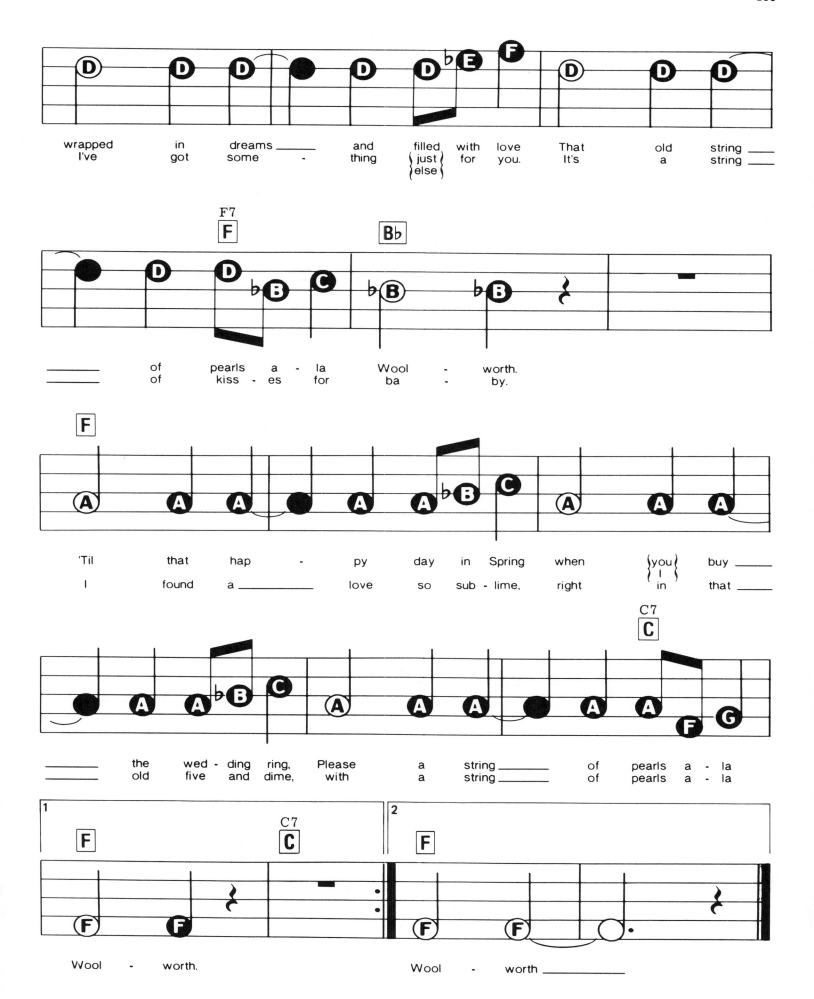

Sentimental Journey

Registration 2
Rhythm: Fox Trot or Swing

By Bud Green,
Les Brown and Ben Homer

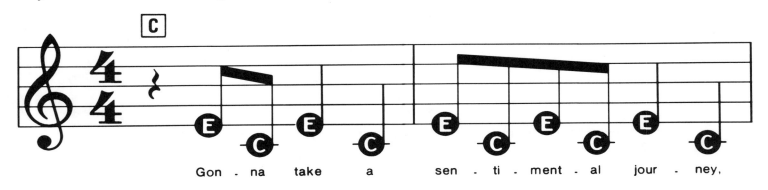

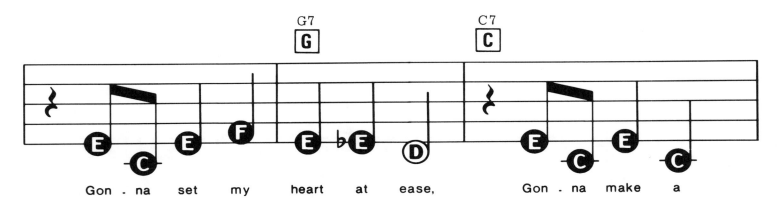

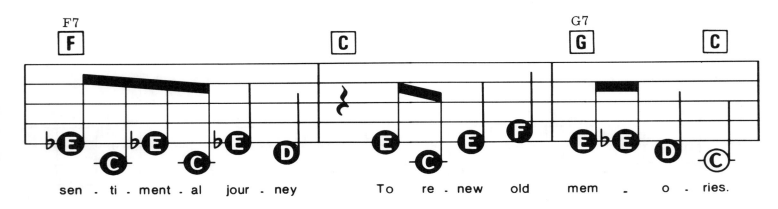

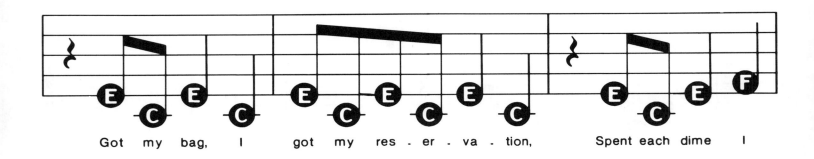

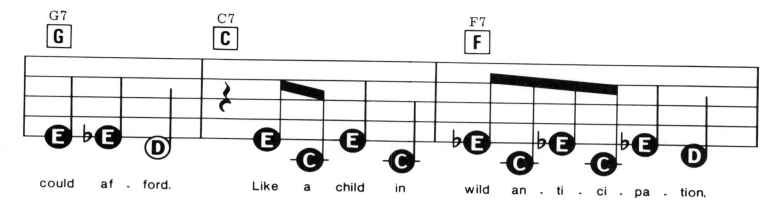

could af - ford.   Like a child in   wild an - ti - ci - pa - tion,

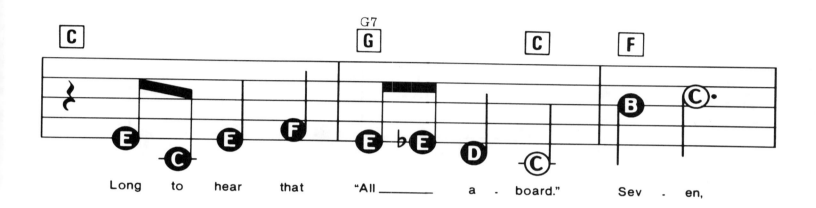

Long to hear that   "All _____ a - board."   Sev - en,

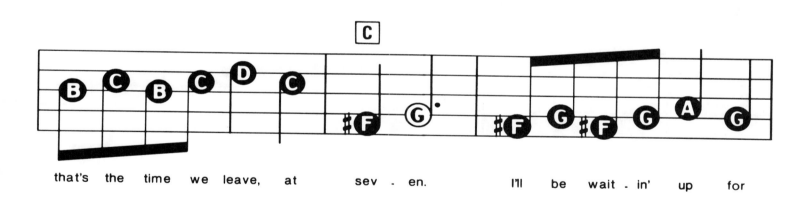

that's the time we leave, at   sev - en.   I'll be wait - in' up for

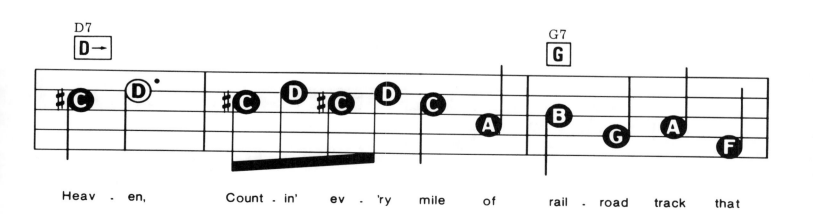

Heav - en,   Count - in' ev - 'ry mile   of   rail - road track   that

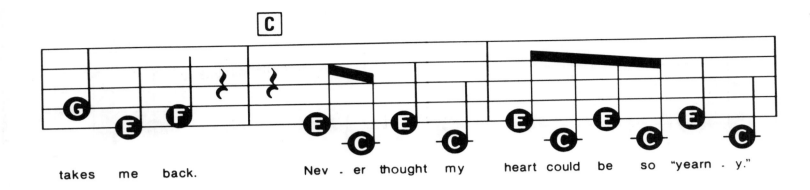

takes me back. Nev - er thought my heart could be so "yearn - y."

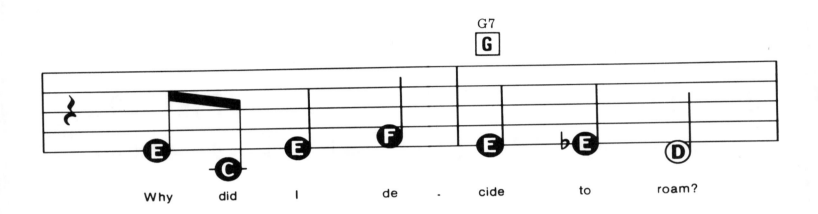

Why did I de - cide to roam?

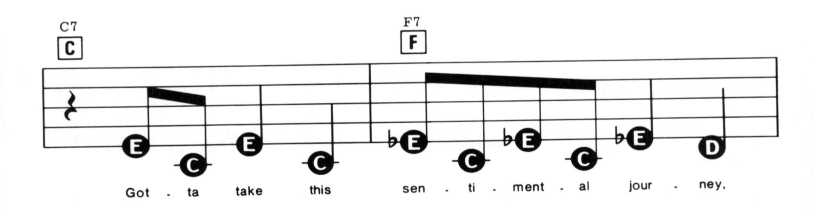

Got - ta take this sen - ti - ment - al jour - ney,

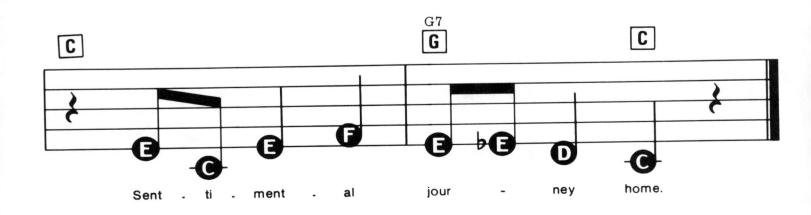

Sent - i - ment - al jour - ney home.

There's A Star Spangled Banner Waving Somewhere

Registration 7
Rhythm: Country or Swing

Words and Music by Paul Roberts
and Shelby Darnell

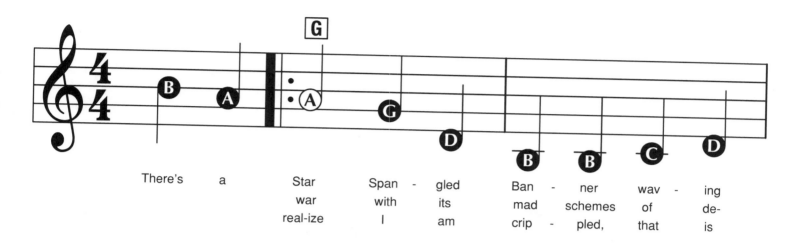

There's	a	Star	Span	-	gled	Ban	-	ner	wav	-	ing
		war	with		its	mad		schemes	of		de-
		real-ize	I		am	crip	-	pled,	that		is

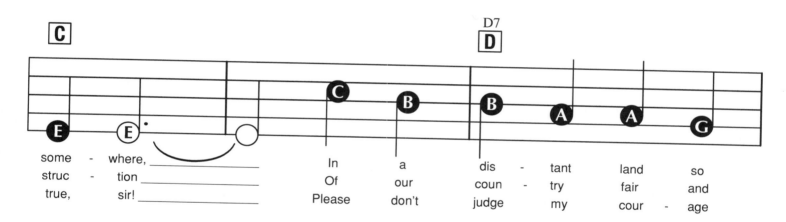

some	-	where, _____		In	a	dis	-	tant	land	so
struc	-	tion _____		Of	our	coun	-	try	fair	and
true,		sir! _____		Please	don't	judge	my	cour	-	age

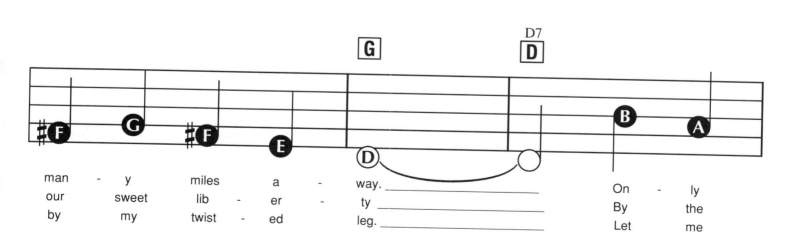

man	-	y	miles	a	-	way. _____		On	-	ly
our		sweet	lib	-	er	-	ty _____		By	the
by		my	twist	-	ed		leg. _____		Let	me

114

That Old Black Magic
from the Paramount Picture STAR SPANGLED RHYTHM

Words by Johnny Mercer
Music by Harold Arlen

Registration 1
Rhythm: Fox Trot or Swing

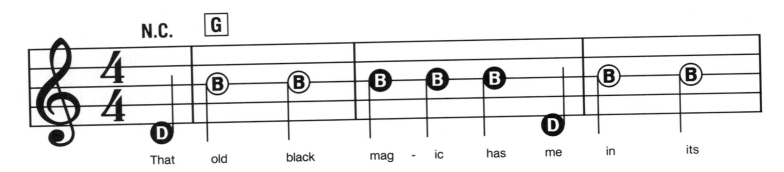

That   old   black   mag - ic   has   me   in   its

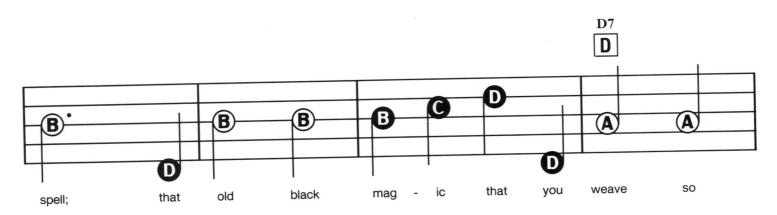

spell;   that   old   black   mag - ic   that   you   weave   so

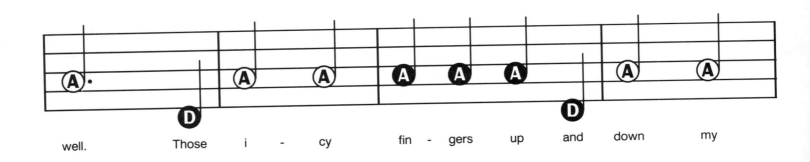

well.   Those   i - cy   fin - gers   up   and   down   my

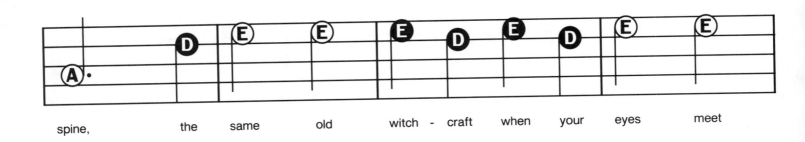

spine,   the   same   old   witch - craft   when   your   eyes   meet

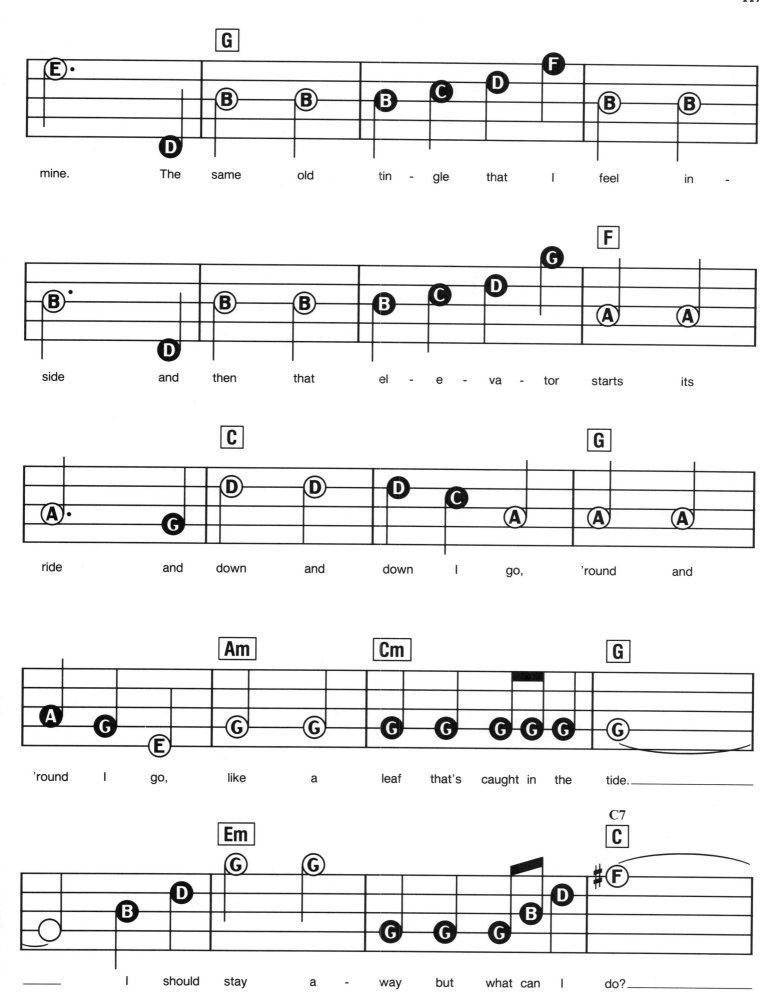

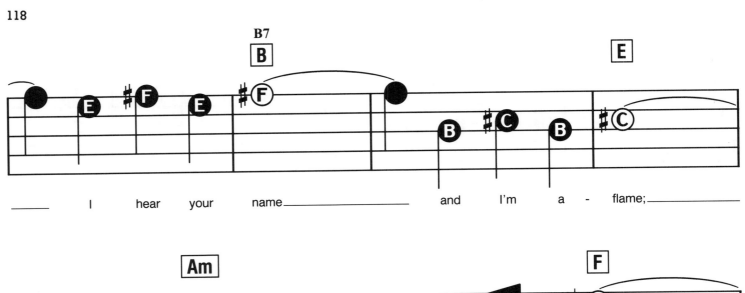

I hear your name_____ and I'm a - flame;_____

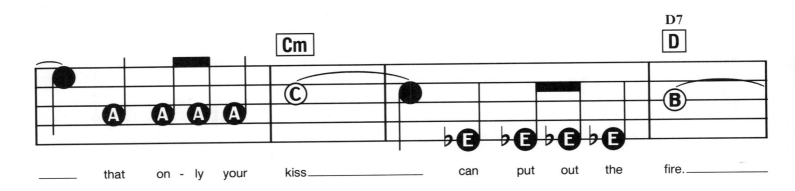

a - flame with such a burn - ing de - sire_____

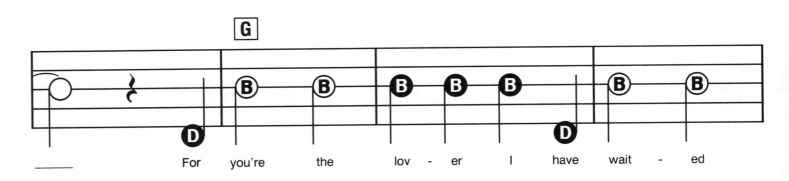

_____ that on - ly your kiss_____ can put out the fire._____

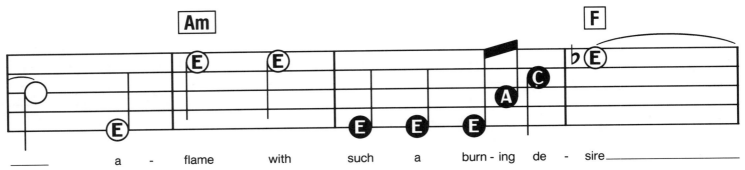

_____ For you're the lov - er I have wait - ed

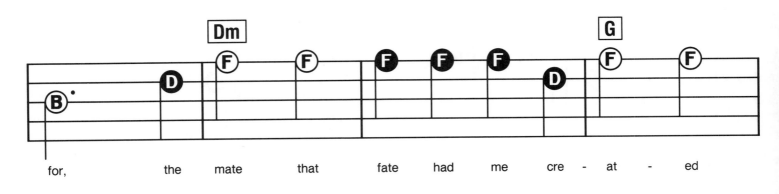

for, the mate that fate had me cre - at - ed

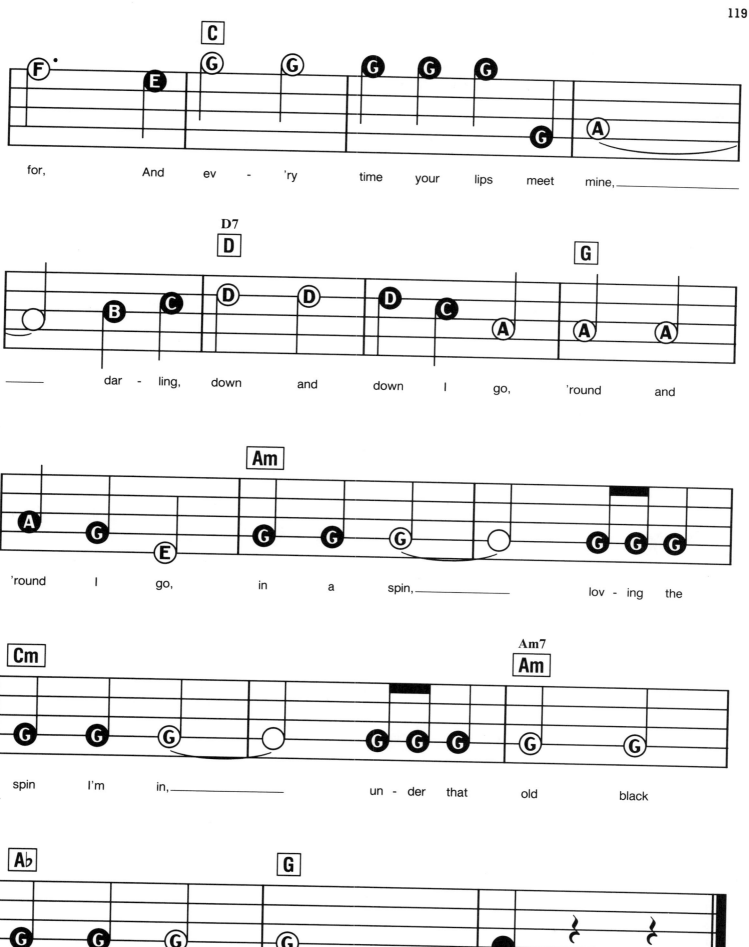

This Is My Country

Registration 10
Rhythm: Fox Trot or Swing

Words by Don Raye
Music by Al Jacobs

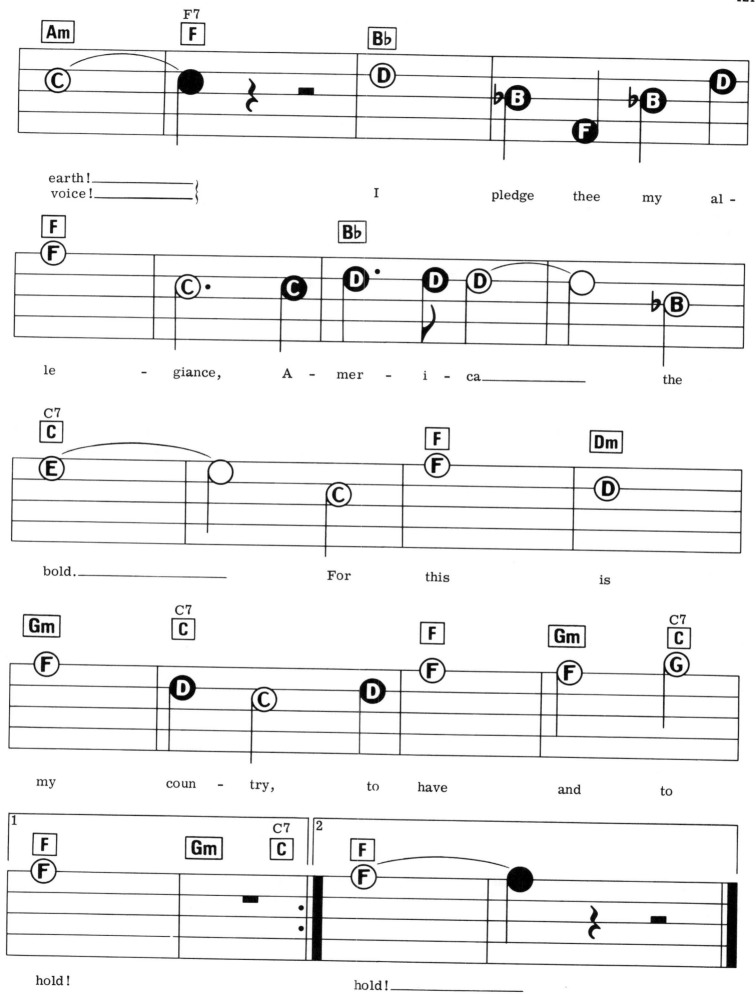

earth!_____
voice!_____
I pledge thee my al -

le - giance, A - mer - i - ca_____ the

bold._____ For this is

my coun - try, to have and to

hold!

hold!_____

They're Either Too Young Or Too Old

Registration 5
Rhythm: Fox Trot or Swing

Words by Frank Loesser
Music by Arthur Schwartz

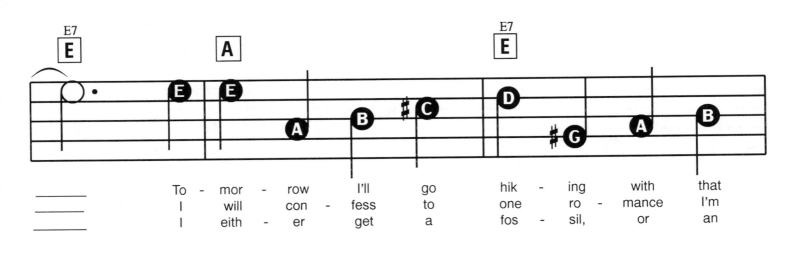

To - mor - row I'll go hik - ing with that
I will con - fess to one ro - mance that I'm
I eith - er get a fos - sil, or an

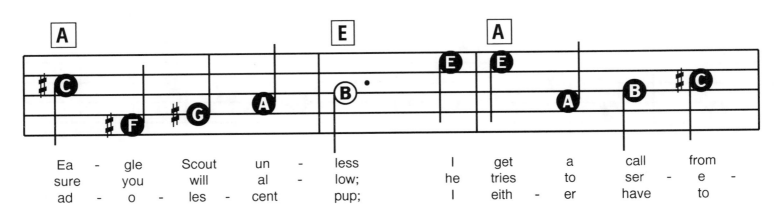

Ea - gle Scout un - less I get a call from
sure you will al - low; he tries to ser - e -
ad - o - les - cent pup; I eith - er have to

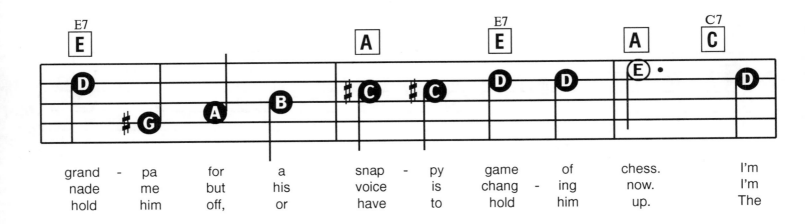

grand - pa for a snap - py game of chess. I'm
nade me for but his voice is chang - ing now. I'm
hold him off, or have to hold him up. The

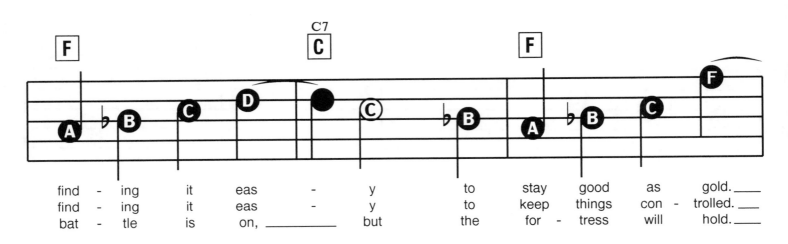

find - ing it eas - y to stay good as gold. ____
find - ing it eas - y to keep things con - trolled. ____
bat - tle is on, _____ but the for - tress will hold. ____

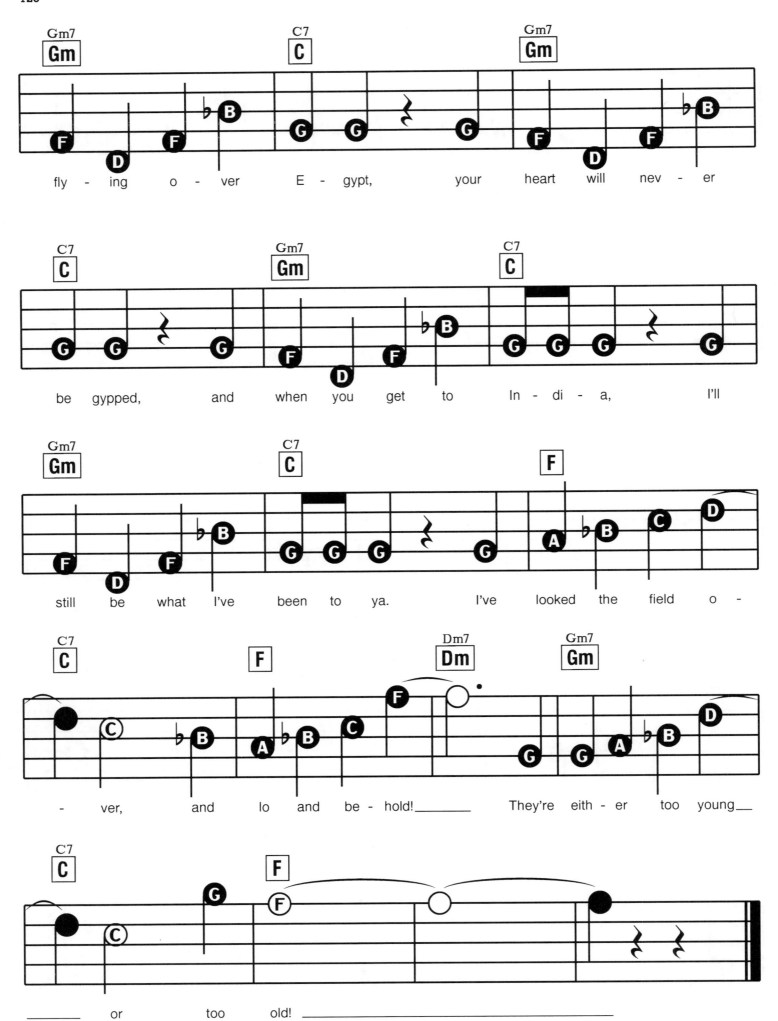

What Do You Do In The Infantry

Registration 5
Rhythm: 6/8 March

By Frank Loesser

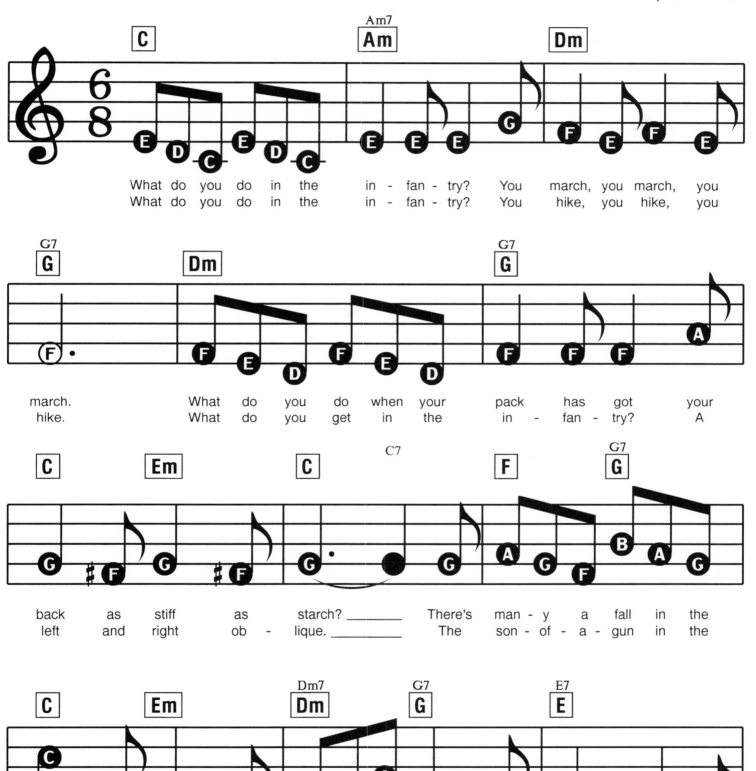

When The Lights Go On Again
(All Over The World)

Registration 7
Rhythm: Ballad

Words and Music by Eddie Seiler,
Sol Marcus and Bennie Benjamin

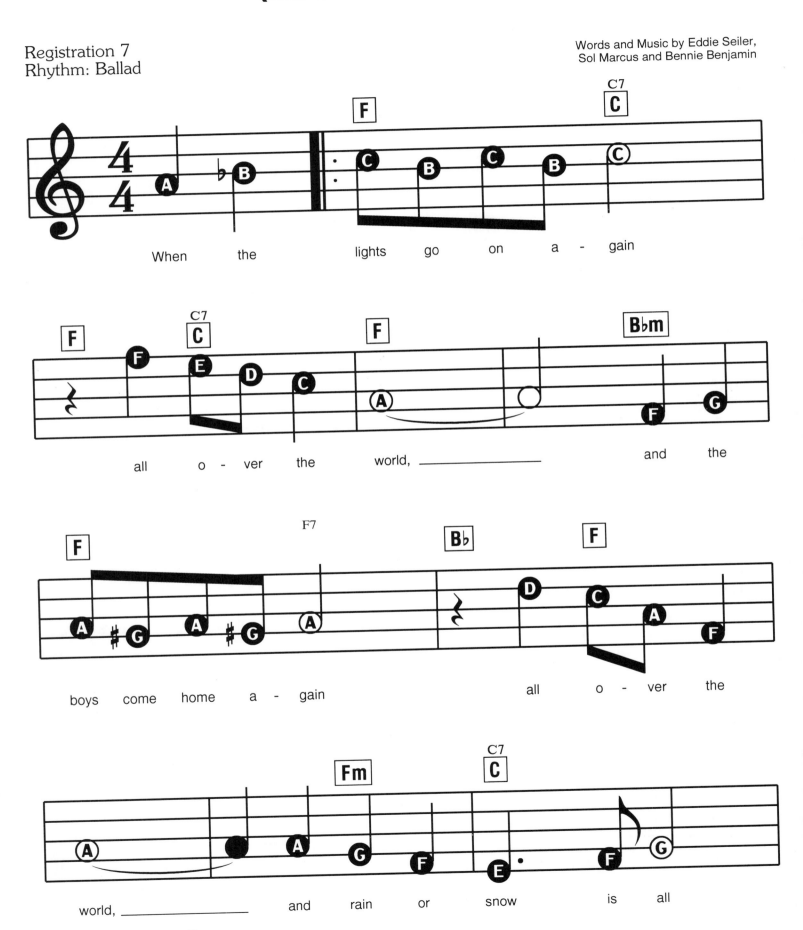

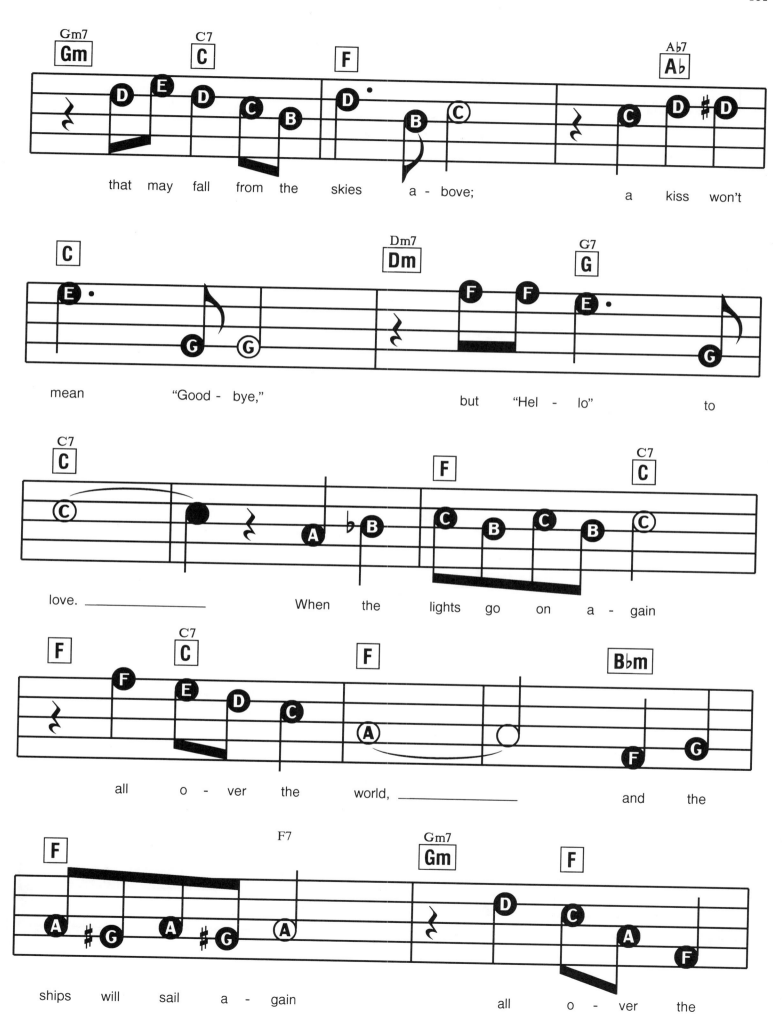

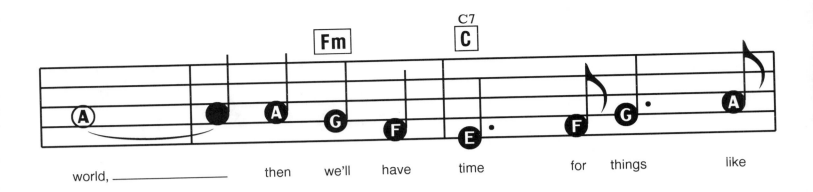

world, _____ then we'll have time for things like

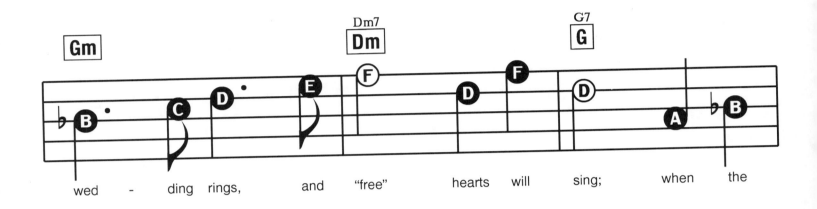

wed - ding rings, and "free" hearts will sing; when the

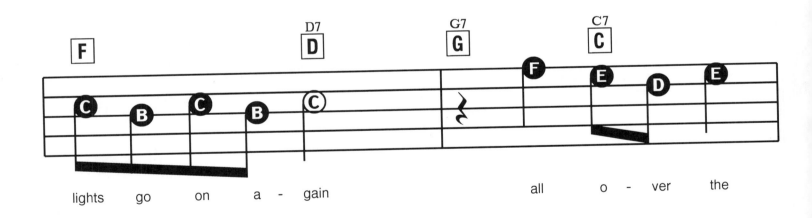

lights go on a - gain all o - ver the

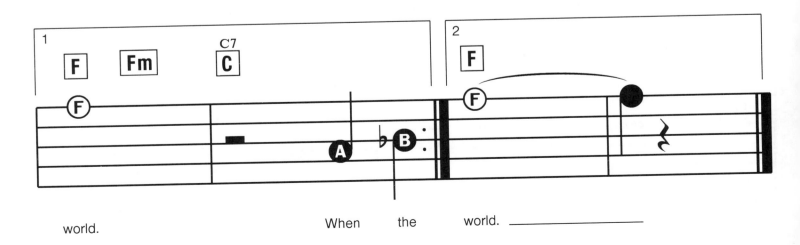

world.   When the world. _____

(There'll Be Bluebirds Over)
The White Cliffs Of Dover

Registration 3
Rhythm: Fox Trot or Swing

Words by Nat Burton
Music by Walter Kent

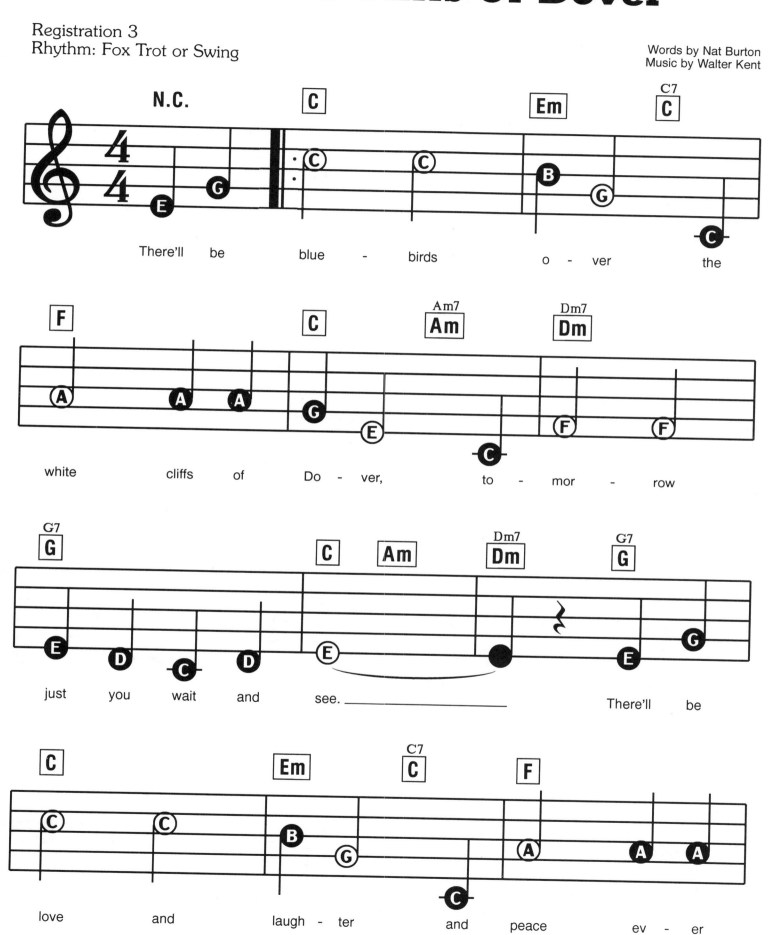

134

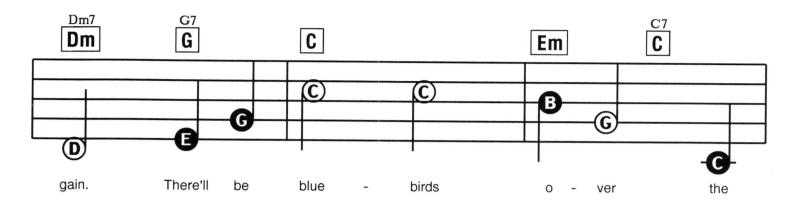

gain.   There'll   be   blue - birds   o - ver   the

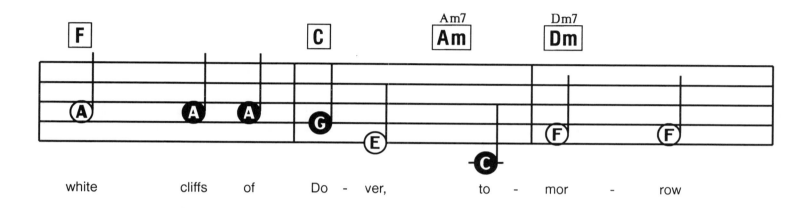

white   cliffs   of   Do - ver,   to - mor - row

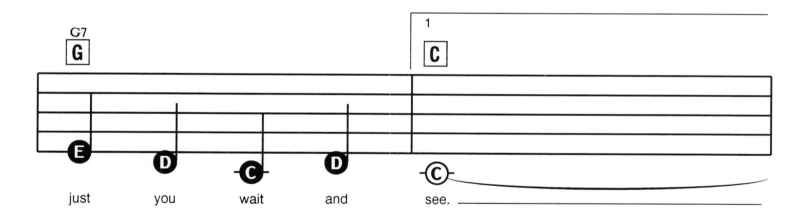

just   you   wait   and   see. _____

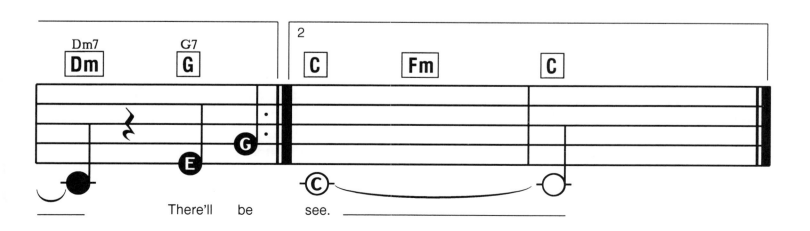

There'll be   see. _____

Why Do They Call A Private A Private?

from the Army Special Services Revue ABOUT FACE

Registration 1
Rhythm: Shuffle or Swing

By Frank Loesser
and Peter Lind Hayes

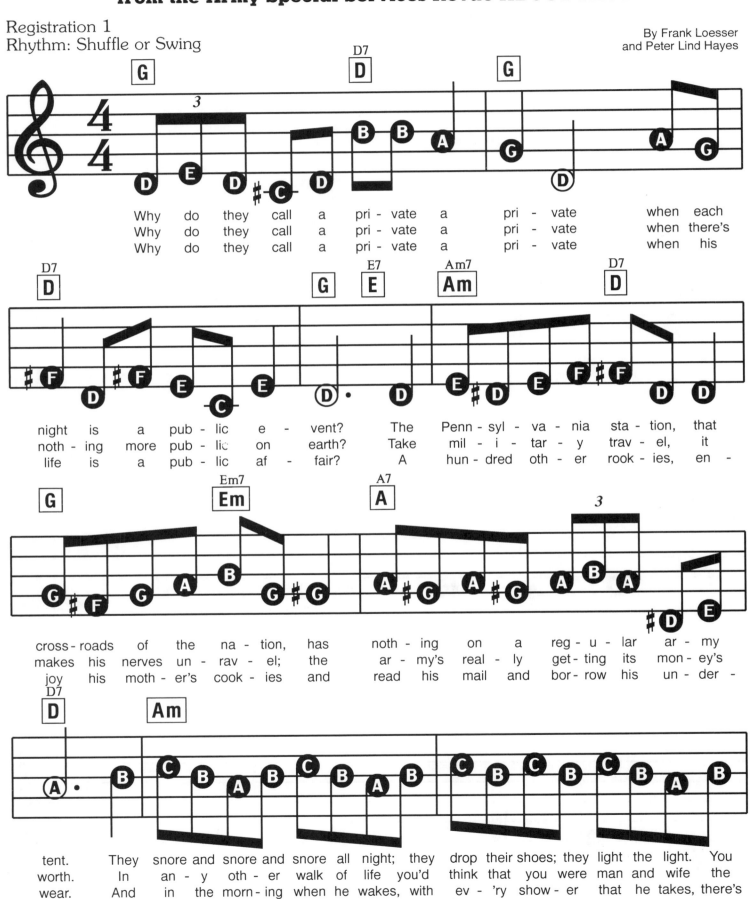

You And I

Registration 4
Rhythm: Fox Trot or Swing

Words and Music by
Meredith Willson

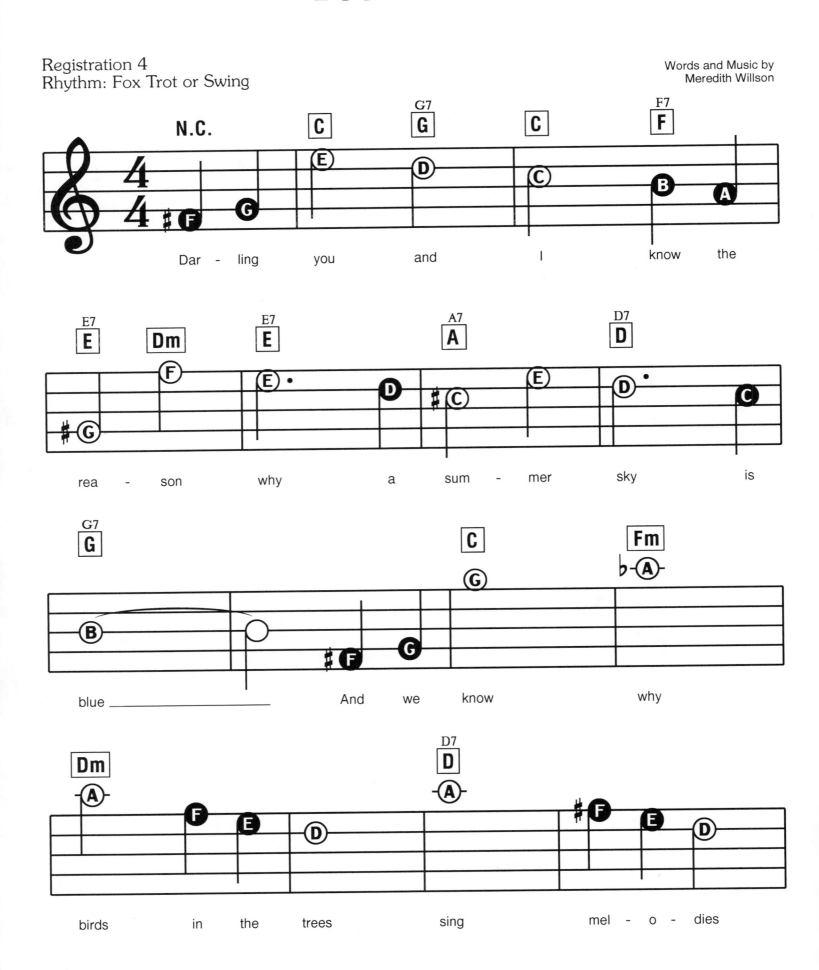

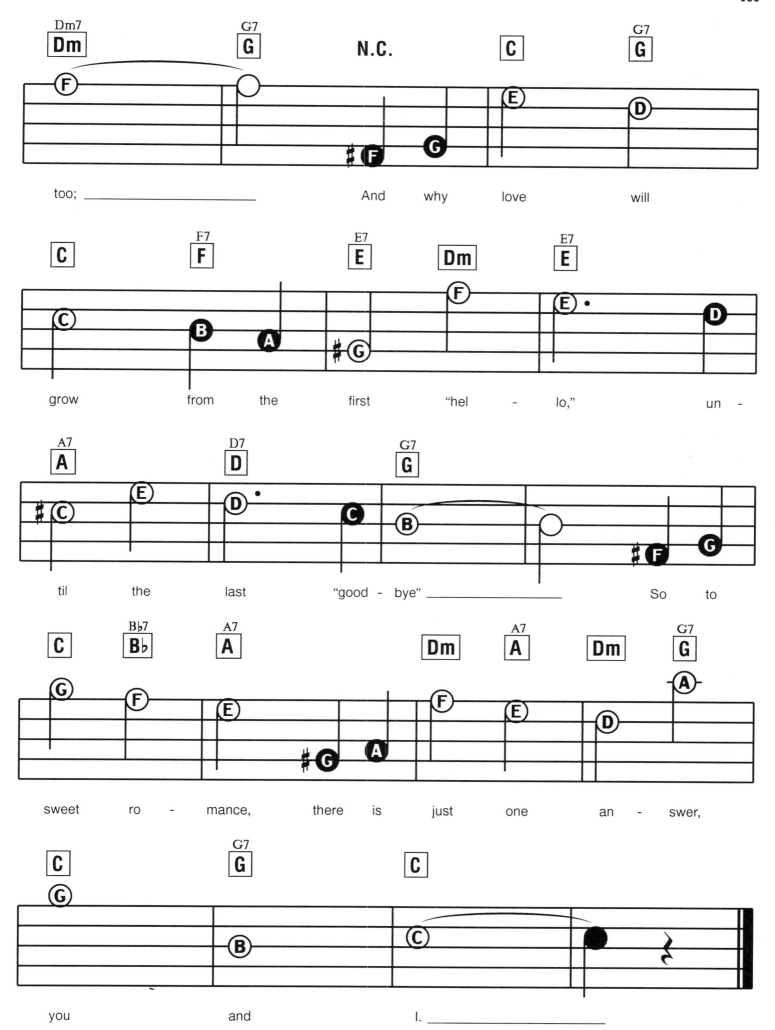

You'd Be So Nice To Come Home To

from SOMETHING TO SHOUT ABOUT

Registration 9
Rhythm: Swing

Words and Music by
Cole Porter

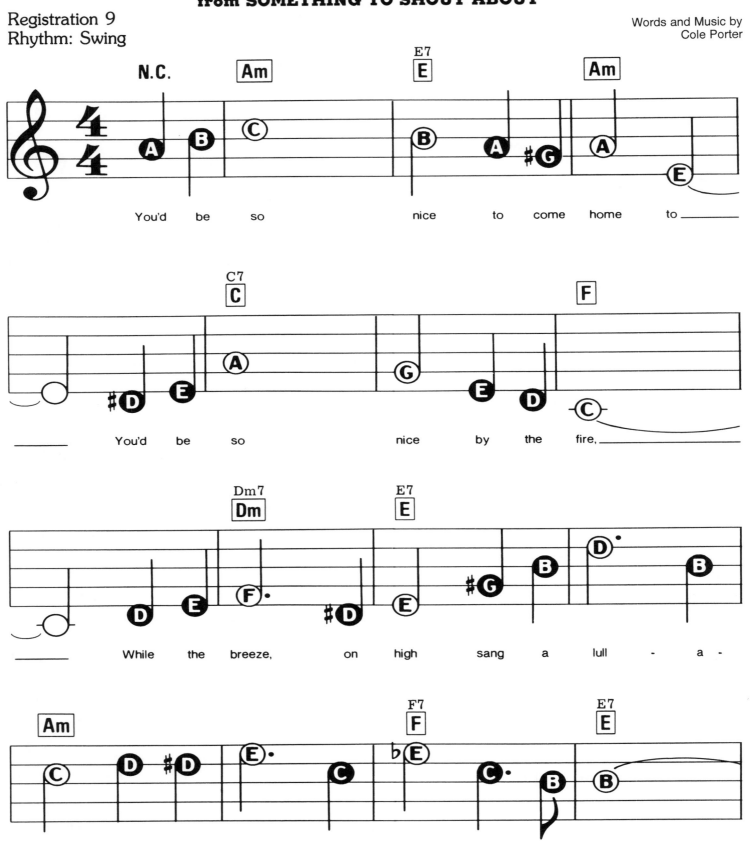

You'll Never Know

Registration 10
Rhythm: Slow Rock or Ballad

Words by Mack Gordon
Music by Harry Warren

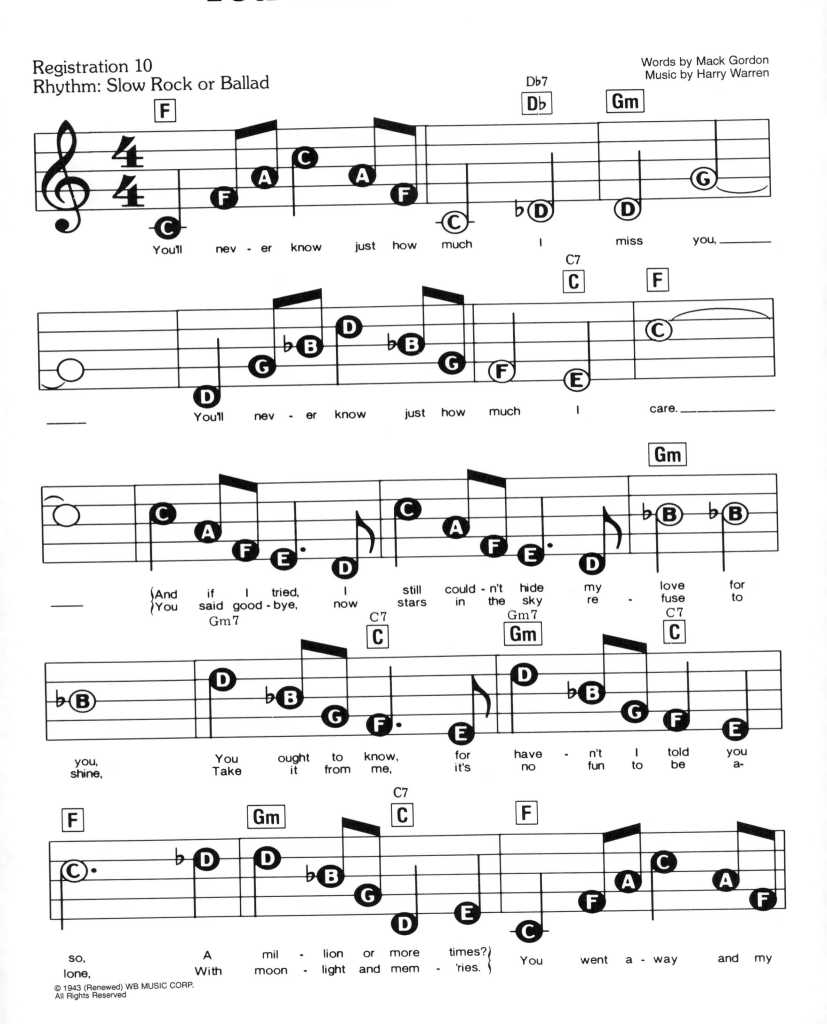

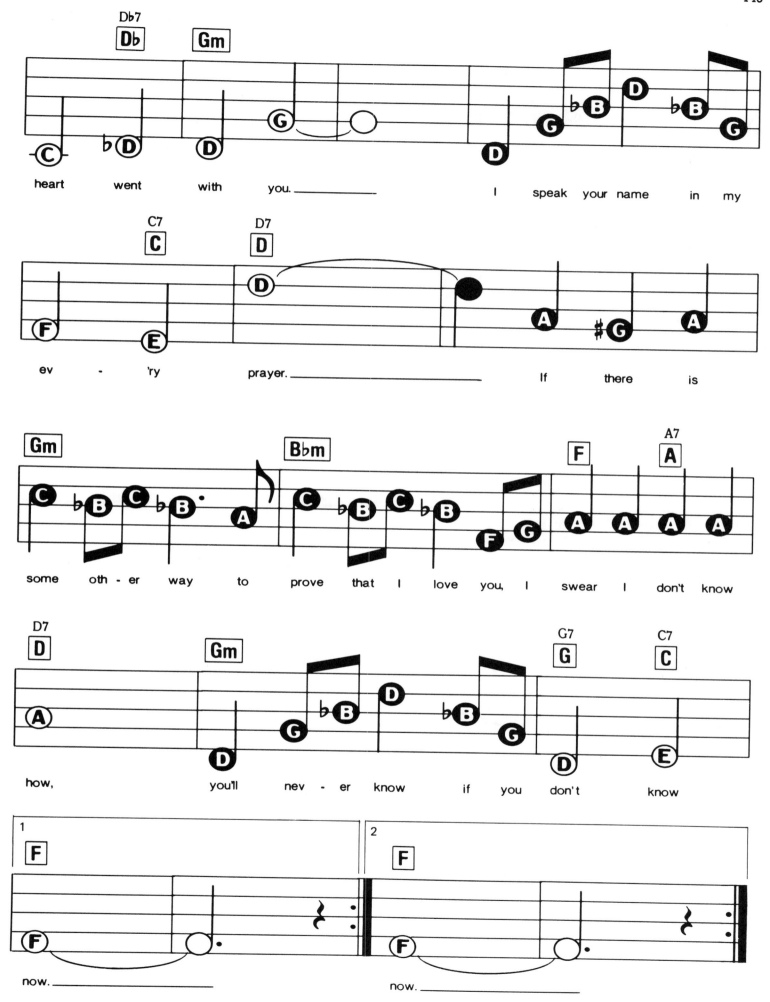

Registration Guide

- Match the Registration number on the song to the corresponding numbered category below. Select and activate an instrumental sound available on your instrument.
- Choose an automatic rhythm appropriate to the mood and style of the song. (Consult your Owner's Guide for proper operation of automatic rhythm features.)
- Adjust the tempo and volume controls to comfortable settings.

Registration

1	Flute, Pan Flute, Jazz Flute
2	Clarinet, Organ
3	Violin, Strings
4	Brass, Trumpet, Bass
5	Synth Ensemble, Accordion, Brass
6	Pipe Organ, Harpsichord
7	Jazz Organ, Vibraphone, Vibes, Electric Piano, Jazz Guitar
8	Piano, Electric Piano
9	Trumpet, Trombone, Clarinet, Saxophone, Oboe
10	Violin, Cello, Strings